# DESIGNS FOR BARGELLO

# DESIGNS FOR Bargello

62 ORIGINAL PATTERNS INSPIRED
BY OR ADAPTED FROM A RANGE
OF HISTORICAL AND CULTURAL
SOURCES ✍ BY NIKKI SCHEUER
PHOTOGRAPHED BY JERRY ROSEN

DOUBLEDAY & COMPANY, INC., GARDEN CITY, NEW YORK 1973

*To My Beloved Family*

ACKNOWLEDGMENTS

My deep gratitude to Margery Kahn, first because she introduced me to Bargello, then for joining me in doing some of the research for this book (she found designs no. 11 and 55, found and adapted designs no. 4, 20, 33, 36, 58), finally for her great encouragement right from the outset of this project.

I thank my daughter Eve, age eleven, for finding design no. 44, for executing design no. 29 and also for testing out my directions.

I thank my son Marc, age sixteen, for reading the manuscript and making suggestions.

My great appreciation to Jean Mailey, head of the Textile Study Room of the Metropolitan Museum of Art, for allowing me free access to the resources of her department.

My gratitude to Anne Winter, Berta Kaslow and Bobby Solow for reading the written material of this book.

My appreciation to Helene Silvan, Marge Scheuer, Pat Daniels and Marion Steinberg for suggestions and encouragement.

My thanks to Sue Koestler, my neighborhood supplier, who sold me supplies whenever I needed them, day or night.

My thanks to my editor Elsa van Bergen, for her faith in and efforts on behalf of this project.

Lastly, my eternal thanks to my photographer, Jerry Rosen, for his superb photographs.

PROJECT ACKNOWLEDGMENTS

Projects made and lent by:
    Marion Steinberg—pillows, designs no. 12 and 44.
    Joy Pack—pillow, design no. 2; belt, design no. 37.
    Betty Osman—telephone book cover, design no. 62.
                  tennis racket cover, design no. 56.
    Betty Serrano—belt, design no. 36.

Photographs of Source Pieces
    Hans Scherr-Thoss, source for designs no. 11 and 55.
    American Museum of Natural History, source for designs 48 and 50.
    Museum of Primitive Art, New York, source for design no. 2.
    Metropolitan Museum of Art, source for design no. 15.

Bargello embroidery is based upon repetitive geometric arrangements, which are worked on canvas in vertical stitches of varying lengths usually covering an even number of canvas threads.

Bargello (also called Florentine needlework) has become the popular name for this type of needlepoint, probably because there are a set of chairs covered with this kind of embroidery in the Bargello Museum, in Florence, Italy. Actually, needlework of this type dates back to the Middle Ages and possibly earlier.

Bargello is a useful name as it encompasses the following kinds of stitches as well: Hungarian Point, Flame, Brick and Straight Gobelin.

The drawback to Bargello has been the limited resources for patterns to work from, and thus far the historical designs available have almost always been based on Italian, English and American seventeenth- to nineteenth-century *needlepoint* patterns.

I have found that I could adapt into Bargello an almost infinite number of designs from other art forms as well as from different periods of time and cultures.

My book, therefore, offers an entirely new and creative source of over sixty exciting patterns for those already making Bargello, as well as for those just starting. From my designs you can make variations or try new color combinations; in other words, have fun.

Why Bargello? Because to me it is the most gratifying of all the popular forms of needlepoint. In standard needlepoint, whether you use the Continental, Basketweave or other stitch, the design is drawn on the canvas, usually in color, demanding only the patience to fill in with wool stitching the design already there. In Bargello you are quickly able to see the design develop right before your eyes simply by counting the stitches to create the pattern. It is also much less costly, as you don't use a painted canvas.

I have spent hundreds of hours researching historical designs from such art forms as architecture, mosaic, lace, textiles, paintings, etc., to create new designs for Bargello embroidery. A few of the sources for these are:

New Zealand (Maori) interwoven reeds
Turkish brickwork of the thirteenth century
Egyptian painting of the Vth Dynasty
East African woven raffia, circa 1700, from the Bushonga tribe
Pre-Columbian tapestry
European designs of different centuries

(Illustrations of some of these sources can be found on pages 140–143.)

In my research I also discovered the universality of many of the designs. They actually reappear at different times, in different cultures and in different art forms.

First, I transposed my findings into drawings, which often meant working from very tiny examples. Then, I adapted the drawings into needlework using Bargello, the Florentine Stitch technique. This meant spending many hours working out the proper combination of stitches so that it would be easy for needleworkers to follow each design.

At the present time when the machine dominates our culture, many individuals want to work with their hands. We are experiencing a great revival of interest in needlework in particular. Most people, after making their first Bargello, develop a great enthusiasm for it. There is a tremendous feeling of accomplishment and gratification in the whole process of making and completing each design.

Embroidery is one of the oldest arts. Most embroidery in Europe and America is produced by women, but in the Orient and in medieval Europe it was frequently done by men. As a matter of fact, the Broderers' Company held an honored place among the guilds, and today many men have turned to needlework as a form of creation, expression and relaxation.

## PROJECTS

This is a list of suggested projects ideally suited for needlework.

FOR THE HOME

| | |
|---|---|
| Pillows | Window panels |
| Upholstery—chairs, ottomans, foot stools, benches, cornices, etc. | Wall hangings |
| | Decorative screens |
| Table tops | Rugs (use Paternayan rug yarn) |

Belts—Design 33 and 35

Vest—Design 42

Desk Blotter—Design 32
Frame—Design 31
Eyeglass Case—Design 30
Telephone Book Cover—Design 62

CLOTHING

Vests—men and
    women
Boleros
Pockets and collars
Panels, inserts and
    borders

Wallets and checkbook covers

Hat or headbands
Belts or cummerbunds
Slippers

Handbags—from
    evening to tote size

Suspenders

MISCELLANEOUS

Picture or mirror frame
Eyeglass case
Covers—photo album,
    writing case,
    telephone book,
    appointment book
Panel—attaché case
Pincushion
Doorstop

Bookmark
Tennis racket cover
Typewriter cover



Desk blotter sides
Boxes
Coasters

Plus any other ideas you can think up.

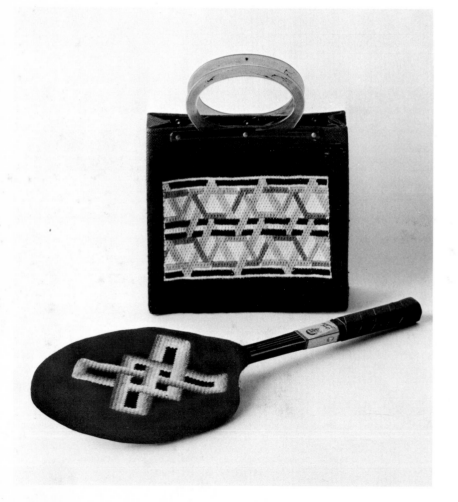

## SELECTING THE DESIGN

This book has been divided into sections of medium-, small- and large-scale designs.

The medium-scale designs are classified into easy, intermediate and advanced groups. Within the small- and large-scale sections, each design is also classified. Don't feel inhibited by the designations. They are only a guide.

If you have never done Bargello before, start with a small-size project (e.g., a small pillow) in an easy design. Bargello work moves quickly. You will be pleased with your accomplishment, and you can go on to your next project.

The photographs are all life size (based on a no. 14 canvas).

This should give you a very clear idea as to the scale of design that would be most appropriate for the project you wish to make.

As a rule, small-scale designs are best for small-size projects, and large-scale, on large projects. NOTE: For projects requiring a lot of wear, do not select designs whose stitches cover more than 4 threads.

When selecting a design feel free to use your imagination and make variations.

# CHOOSING THE COLORS

The color section of the book, showing every design in color, should be helpful in making your selection of colors. I have used all types of color combinations (contrasting, similar, etc.), and I've tried to appeal to many tastes.

In the directions for each design, I suggest the number of colors to use and, in many cases, the number of gradations of each color. There is also an occasional comment on color when I feel it is pertinent.

A design has a different appearance each time another combination of colors is used, and there are many possible combinations. Don't be afraid —experiment until you find the combination that most pleases you.

SUGGESTION: Start a sampler or make a very small sample. For a diamond-type design, make the size of one enclosure. For a linear pattern, make one complete ascent or descent. Use the colors you have chosen, in the order you wish them worked. This then would be your color guide when making your design.

Here are a few thoughts about color and its use.

Color can visually alter the proportion of the design.

A color will change depending on what color surrounds it. For example, when you surround a light bright grade of one color with a very dark grade of another color, or black, this creates a very dynamic effect. See design no. 59.

Contrasting colors will appear to be more brilliant than similar colors, and if one of the two contrasting colors is of a lighter tone, the other color will appear to be even brighter, for example royal blue next to a light red will appear much brighter than royal blue next to a green of the same strength.

Two similar colors of the same intensity used next to each other create a vibrating effect, as is the case with red next to an orange of the same strength.

The use of gradations of the same color produces a soothing effect.

To achieve a lovely textured effect when covering a good bit of the canvas with one color, take one single strand from each of three gradations of the same color and combine them (this can only be done with Paternayan yarn) to derive a beautiful multishaded tone.

Your possibilities are limitless and are, of course, a matter of taste.

# MATERIALS

Use only a good-quality canvas and yarn. It will be easier to work with, look better, last much longer and the difference in cost is not that great.

## CANVAS

For the finest Bargello work in terms of appearance and durability, I suggest you use a no. 14 canvas (14 holes to the inch). One can also use a no. 12 canvas, especially if the stitch length of the design covers less than 4 threads.

Though the work goes more quickly with a larger-hole canvas, it will not wear as well. The designs will also enlarge.

I use only mono canvas (single thread). I prefer it to be white since it is easier on the eyes as you follow the count of the design.

## YARN

I recommend using only Paterna-Persian type and tapestry yarn, or if you can find it, crewel yarn.

If you are looking for an overall effect, rich in texture and color to give life to your design, I think the Persian type, Paternayan yarn (used in all three strands on a no. 14 or no. 12 canvas), is best. It is also a very strong yarn.

If you are more interested in showing the quality of the workmanship (each stitch standing out) and like a soft look with little texture, then I suggest a thinner tapestry yarn. Do not use them on less than a no. 14 canvas.

The amounts of yarn needed for a project using Paternayan yarn are figured as follows:

To cover one square inch of canvas you need 1½ strands of yarn (each strand 24 inches long). There are 48 strands to the ounce. So, to make a piece 12 × 12 inches, it would take about five ounces of yarn (always allow about 10 per cent extra).

You will find most local needlework shops helpful in figuring out the various amounts of yarn you will need. It is better to get a little extra as you sometimes run into a problem of the dye lot being different. The yarn is not that expensive, and if you collect a lot of leftover wool, try using it in making design no. 46.

Keep your yarn in plastic bags so that it will stay clean.

NEEDLES

Use only blunt-end tapestry needles. For Paternayan yarn (using all three strands) use no. 19. For other tapestry yarns—coarser ones, use no. 19; finer ones, use no. 20.

MISCELLANEOUS

Two pairs of scissors. A small very sharp-pointed pair to cut out any errors and to cut the yarn (some people use a ripper to cut out errors). A large pair to cut the canvas.

Needlework bag—something large enough to hold your canvas and yarn. (I tie my small scissors to the handle of my bag with a long ribbon, so I don't misplace them).

Masking tape—to cover the edges of your canvas (available at paint and hardware stores).

Waterproof felt-tip marker—use a light color (yellow) to draw the shape of your project on the canvas.

## PREPARING THE CANVAS FOR WORK

1. To determine the size of the canvas needed, before cutting, follow these guidelines:

For a pillow, upholstery, etc., make an additional inch of work beyond what will be seen.

Always allow for a two-inch canvas margin all around.

Regardless of the shape of your project, work on a squared off canvas.

You are now ready to cut your canvas.

2. Mark off the area of the canvas to be covered with a waterproof marker. If your project requires a pattern, be sure it is the exact size needed.

3. Cover the edges of the canvas with masking tape.

4. Fold the canvas in half, both horizontally and vertically. Where they intersect is the exact center of the canvas. Most designs are started at this point.

5. Thread your needle. Take the end of your yarn (about 2 inches' worth) and loop it around your needle. Pinch the needle and yarn together very tightly. Pull out the needle. Expose a bit of the loop and force the eye of the needle between the pinched fingers and around the yarn. *Voila*, it is threaded. This may take a bit of practice. Never wet the wool.

6. Make your first stitch. Leave about 1 inch of the yarn on the back of your canvas, hold it with your finger and work your next few stitches to cover it. Never make a knot. It will create a bump. In ending or starting a new strand, slip the yarn under the backs of the closest group of stitches.

## MAKING THE OUTLINE

The outline is the line that defines the pattern.

1. It is important to have peace and quiet when making your outline because it requires your complete attention. If you make a mistake and don't correct it, you will keep repeating this error. Establishing the outline is not at all time consuming, and you will then be able to divide your attention when making the rest of the design.

A quick way to check the outline count is to see that the end of each ascent or descent is in line with the adjoining motif, both horizontally and vertically.

Make stitches evenly; if you pull them too tightly the canvas will show through.

2. You usually work your design horizontally from the center of your canvas. Then work above or below.

3. Many people find it easier, when having completed a row, to turn their canvas upside down so that they are always stitching in one direction. Right-handed people go from right to left.

4. To avoid a miscount, it is safest to make your outlines over the entire canvas first.

## FILLING IN THE OUTLINE (usually a repeat of the outline)

1. In a self-enclosed pattern (such as a diamond) fill in one section as a guide for color, if you have not made a sample.

2. There is great leeway in how one goes about filling in the outline on the canvas. Much depends on one's temperament.

You can work each color separately over the entire canvas or, if that is a bit disciplined, fill each enclosure before going on to the next, or do a bit of each.

## FINISHING THE DESIGN

1. To achieve the horizontal line at the top and bottom edge (*see illustration below*): Make one top (or bottom) stitch full length, and the one next to it half that length. Keep alternating in this way.

2. When making most small items add only a few stitches. Too wide an addition will make too thick an overlap.

3. Snip off any extra long threads on the back, leaving about ½ to 1 inch.

Your project is now ready for blocking and mounting. NOTE: Bargello does not pull the canvas out of shape as much as other forms of needlepoint. Therefore, it is not always necessary to block your work. Press it instead. You do this by laying your Bargello face down on a clean smoothly

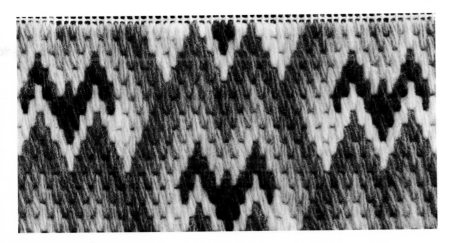

padded ironing board. Take a clean wet cloth, that has been thoroughly wrung out, and cover your work. Press it with a dry iron.

## TIPS

1. Use a strand of yarn no more than 24 inches long.

2. If your yarn is twisting, let the yarn with the needle dangle straight down from your canvas. When it stops twirling, it's untwisted.

3. If you make an error in the length of a stitch when filling your design, it is possible sometimes to make a stitch over it in the correct length. If the error is a bit larger, carefully snip one wrong stitch on the front of the canvas, and pull out the wool with the end of your needle. Make sure the ends are long enough (about ¾ inch) to slip under the backs of the other stitches. Be cautious about using the yarn you have pulled out. It is frequently weakened, having been rubbed by the canvas. If it is a really sizable mistake, snip carefully all the wrong stitches (on front) and pull the loose threads out (on the back) with your needle or tweezers. Be sure to slip the ends of the yarn under the backs of the stitches.

4. If you accidentally cut your canvas or you must enlarge the area of your canvas, place another piece directly under the cut, or add a piece the desired size. Place one inch of it under your original canvas and sew it in place. Make sure you match up the holes. Then make your needlepoint through both layers of canvas.

5. When making a design with a solid background or frame:
   a. Cover that area of your canvas, in the same or a similar color, with waterproof acrylic or a waterproof felt-tip marker. Otherwise the canvas might show through your work, even when using the right weight wool and canvas size.
   b. Work the stitches in long diagonal lines. Make the stitches as even as possible to create a smooth effect.

6. When placing a second unconnected motif on your canvas (*see design no. 9*) it is safest to insert the necessary number of stitches between the motifs in a temporary color, rather than counting holes.

7. If your canvas is too large to leave flat when stitching, oll the end you are not working on.

## DESIGN DIRECTIONS

These directions are offered as a tool to help you start and give you guidance in making your design.

For some, the photographs will be self-explanatory. The NOTES, however, might be useful as a few of the designs are more detailed and intricate than they appear to be at first glance.

The center of the photograph is not always in the center of the design, as the photograph is intended to show the repeat of the pattern.

Explanation of terms used are listed below:

### OUTLINE:

In the black-and-white photographs I have deliberately left part of the designs unfinished in order to identify their outline.

### STITCH LENGTH:

This is the number of threads of canvas that your wool covers. NOTE: Your stitches are always vertical.

### STEPS:

Ascending or descending stitches are always a given number of threads of canvas to the immediate right or left of the previous stitch(es).

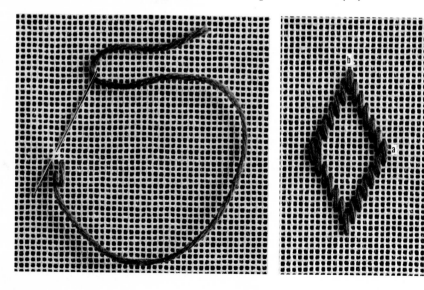

Example: (as listed in directions)

"stitch length: covering 4 threads"

"steps: up or down 2 threads"

You actually make both the stitch length and step all in one motion (*see illustration below left*).

### TO ASCEND:

Count up 4 threads of canvas. After inserting the needle, step down 2 threads with your eye, turn the needle (on a diagonal) and bring the point toward you through the hole to the immediate right (or left). Pull the needle and yarn through the hole. Start the next stitch.

### TO START:

My suggested starting place indicates where you place the first stitch(es) of your outline on your canvas. The arrow shows this starting place.

In counting a given number of holes from the center, remember hole no. 1 is *next* to the center.

When describing diamond (or self-enclosed) outlines, I use the following terms (*see illustration below right*).

 a. Horizontal point: This is the point that divides the upper half of the outline from the lower half.

 b. Vertical point: This is the top and bottom point of the outline.

 c. Sides: Diagonals going from a. to b. or b. to a.

 d. You will find directions for a given number of stitches ascending and descending each side of the diamond (self-enclosed). The last stitch of one side is counted as the first stitch of the next. Example: "10 sts. asc. and desc. *each side*." Stitch no. 10 counts as stitch no. 1 of the adjoining side.

## ABBREVIATION DEFINITIONS

| | | |
|---|---|---|
| asc. =ascending | grad. =gradations | rt. =right |
| cont. =continue | horiz.=horizontal | st(s).=stitch(es) |
| dbl. =double | lt. =left | vert. =vertical |
| desc. =descending | pt. =point | |

# DESIGNS

# 1 ✍

# ADAPTED FROM JAPANESE
# NINETEENTH-CENTURY STENCIL CUTTING

This marvelous design makes one think of the sea, reflecting the Japanese love of nature.

If you have never done Bargello before, this is a good one with which to begin.

OUTLINE: wave

STITCH LENGTH: cover 4 threads

STEPS: up or down 2 threads

COLORS: 2. 4 grad. of 1st color (1 grade very dark); single grade of 2nd color (light and bright). It is most effective having the light bright color just below the darkest grade of the other color. See color page 71.

A. Start at the mid-point of the right edge of the canvas.

B. Make the 1st row of wave (light bright color) (arrow):

   1. Asc.  lt. 3 singles
              2 doubles
              1 triple
              (top of wave)

|  |  |
|---|---|
| 2. Desc. lt. 2 doubles | 3. Asc. lt. 2 doubles |
| 5 singles | 14 singles |
| 2 doubles | 2 doubles |
| 1 triple | 1 triple |
| (bottom of wave) | (top of wave) |

Repeat 2 and 3 until the row is completed.

C. Make the rows above and below until the canvas is covered.

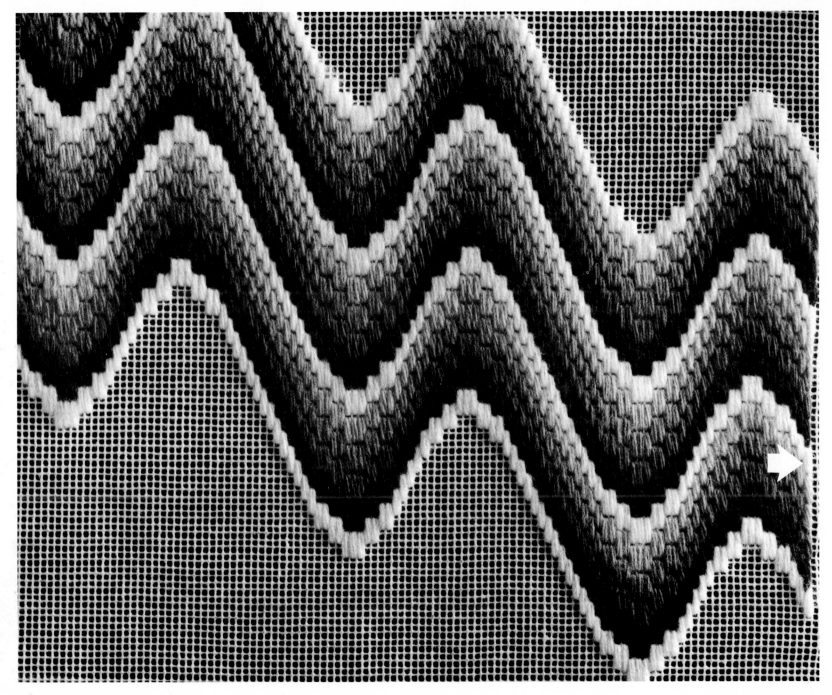

## 2

# ADAPTED FROM INDIAN (ASSAM) TWENTIETH-CENTURY HANDLOOM SHAMBAG

The Nagas of Assam created this interesting design now in the Museum of Primitive Art, New York. (See photo page 142.)

OUTLINE: twin peak diamond
STITCH LENGTH: covering 4 threads
STEPS: up or down 2 threads
COLORS: 2. See color page 67.

A. Start from the center of the canvas, count to the right 15 holes.
B. Make the outline of the top half of a twin peak diamond (arrow). Insert 1st stitch then,

    Asc. lt. 11 sts.
    Desc. lt.  4 sts.
    Asc. lt.  4 sts.
    Desc. lt. 11 sts.     Repeat these across the canvas.

C. From the 1st stitch, repeat B to the right.
D. Turn the canvas upside down, make the bottom half of the design.
E. After completing the outlines of the twin peak diamonds, repeat these rows above and below until the canvas is covered.
F. Fill the twin peak diamonds as shown.

VARIATION: (Shown on p. 2) Change the 7th outline row, above and below the completed design, into an outline of diamonds. Asc. and desc. 12 sts. *each side*. (The diamonds fall between 2 twin peak diamonds.) Continue with rows of diamond outlines, etc. Fill in the remaining areas.

## 3

# ADAPTED FROM FRENCH CIRCA 1925
# DESIGN BY MAURICE DUFRÊNNE

This chic Art Deco design found on a limousine must have caused much discussion.

OUTLINE: inverted letter **V**

STITCH LENGTH: covering 4 threads

STEPS: up or down 2 threads

COLORS: 5. Make the row under the outline darker than the outline and the background light. See color page 79.

A. Start from the center of the canvas, count to the right 13 holes.

B. Make the outline of an inverted V (arrow):

Asc. lt. 8 dbl. sts.

Desc. lt. 7 dbl. sts.

Skip 2 holes (or 8th stitch). Repeat these directions across the canvas.

From the 1st stitch, skip 2 holes, then asc. and desc. right, etc.

C. Make the outline row above: Next to any of the highest points of the previous row, start 1st double stitches and follow from B.

D. Make the outline row below: In any of the 2 holes skipped of the original row, start 1st double stitch, then:

Desc. 8 dbl. sts.

Skip 2 holes.

Then follow B and repeat across the canvas to the left, and then right.

E. Cover the canvas with outlines.

F. Fill in remaining areas as shown.

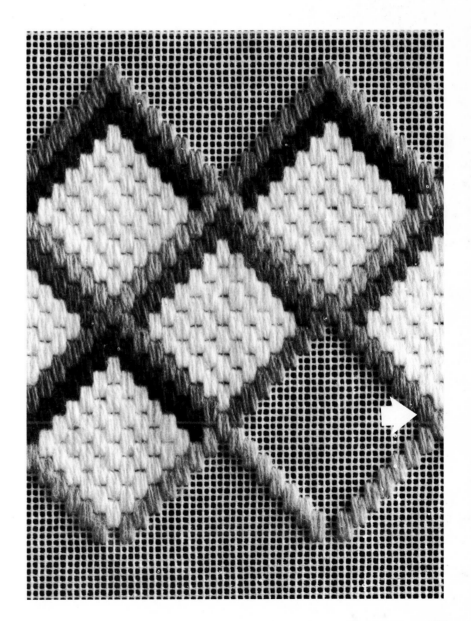

## 4 ✍

## ADAPTED FROM SCANDANAVIAN
## TRADITIONAL KNITTING PATTERN

In this exciting design we have one design superimposed on another.

OUTLINE: diamonds
STITCH LENGTH: covering 2* and 4 threads
STEPS: up or down 2 threads
COLORS: 4. See color page 68.

* The upper right corner of the photograph locates the single stitches and those covering 2 threads.

A. Start from the center of the canvas, count to the right 17 holes.
B. Make the outline of a diamond (arrow):
   Asc. and desc. 10 dbl. sts. *each side*.
C. Make the outline of diamonds across the canvas, to the left and right.
D. Then above and below.
E. Next make the small square motifs in the center of alternating diamonds.
F. Fill in the background squares as shown.

NOTE: The horizontal edge in both the large and small squares is achieved by alternating stitches covering 2 and 4 threads.
   The vertical edge of the large squares is formed by single stitches.

# 5 ✍

# ADAPTED FROM ITALIAN
# SIXTEENTH-CENTURY VELVET

This rich design reminds one of nature; mountain peaks with birds.

OUTLINE: twin peak motifs

STITCH LENGTH: covering 4 threads

STEPS: up or down 2 threads

COLORS: 6. 4 grad. each of 3 colors, plus black and white for accent and contrast. See color page 78.

SPECIAL PROJECTS: this would be beautiful on a vest.

A. Start at the mid-point of the bottom edge of the canvas.

B. Make the outline of a twin peak motif (arrow):
   1. Asc. rt. 10 sts.    3. Asc. rt. 4 sts.
   2. Desc. rt. 4 sts.    4. Desc. rt. 9 sts.

C. Make the outline of the motifs above (to the right and left):
   From the top stitch of either peak in the previous outline, count down 5 stitches. Start the next motif. Follow B, substituting the word left for right, when necessary.

D. Keep building outlines above until canvas is covered.

E. To achieve the outline of the motif below, see photograph.

F. Fill in the remaining areas as shown.

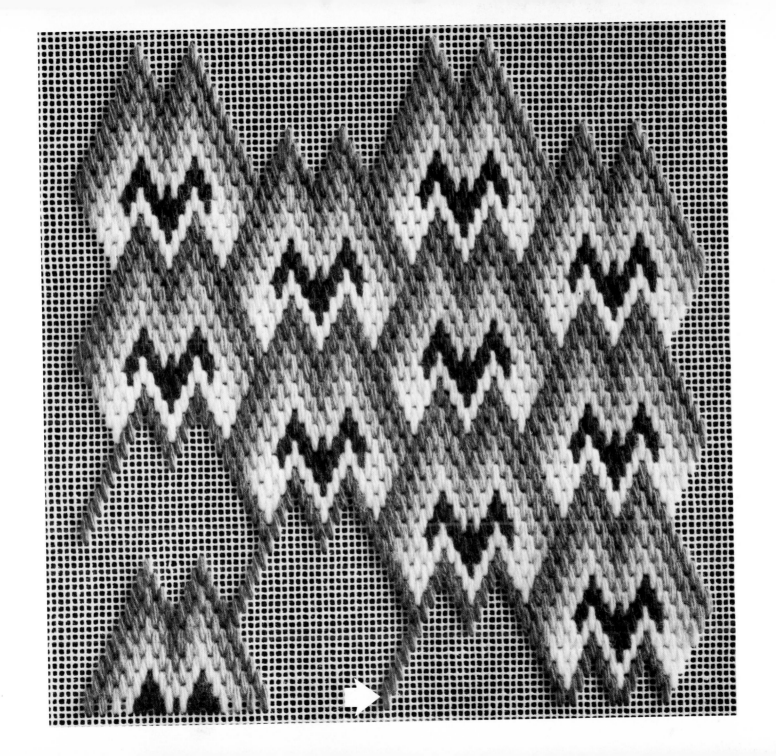

6 ⚞

# ADAPTED FROM ITALIAN (LUCCA)
# EIGHTEENTH-CENTURY SATIN
# WINDOW CURTAINS

This classic flame design is to be found in the Collection of Contessa M. A. Bernadini, Lucca, Italy.

OUTLINE: darkest line shown

STITCH LENGTH: covering 2 and 6 threads

STEPS: up or down 1 thread

COLORS: 3. 4 grad. each of 3 colors. See color page 72.

A. Start at the mid-point of the right edge of the canvas.

B. Make 1st row (arrow):

1st stitch short (2 threads).

| 1. Desc. lt. 2 long sts. (6 threads) | 2. Asc. lt. 2 short sts. |
|---|---|
| 2 short sts. | 2 long sts. |
| 2 long sts. | 2 short sts. |
| 2 short sts. | 2 long sts. |
| 1 long st. | 1 short st. |
| (bottom of outline) | (top of outline) |

Repeat these across the canvas.

CHECK PHOTOGRAPH: The length of the top and bottom stitch is repeated in the next row. The stitch length is reversed in the following 2 rows, etc.

C. Make the rows above and below until the canvas is covered.

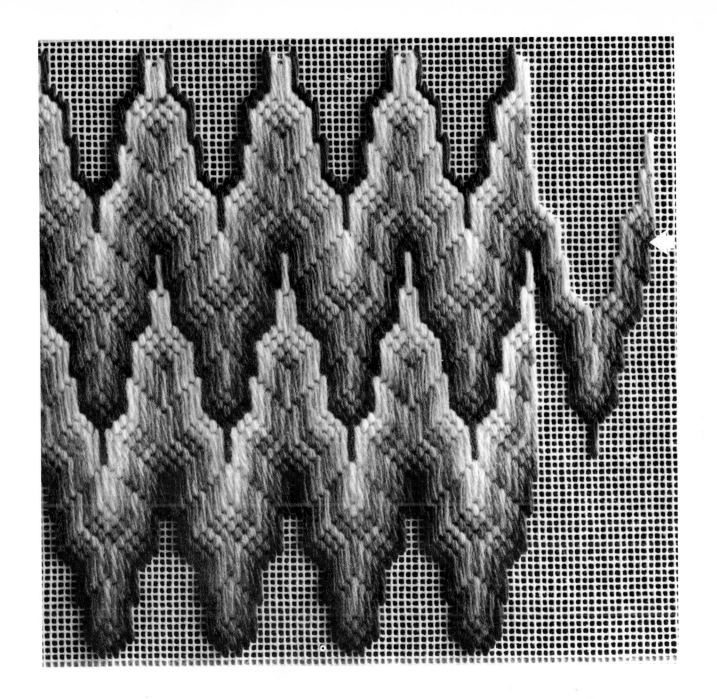

# 7 ✒

# ADAPTED FROM AFGHANISTAN
# NINETEENTH-CENTURY EMBROIDERY

This design, with its grand proportions, was taken from a small purse in the collection of Margery Kahn, New York.

Turn the book around so that the stitches in the photograph are vertical.

OUTLINE: large and small diamonds
STITCH LENGTH: covering 4 threads
STEPS: up or down 2 threads
COLORS: 6. See color page 68.

A. Start from the center of the canvas, count to the right 21 holes.
B. Make the outline of a large diamond (arrow):
   Asc. and desc. 22 sts. *each side*.
C. From the 1st stitch, next make the outline of a small diamond:
   Asc. and desc. 7 sts. *each side*.
D. Make large diamonds alternating with small diamonds across the canvas to the left and right.
E. Then above and below until the canvas is covered with outlines.
F. Fill in the twin and small diamonds as shown.
   Note the 3 variations of twin diamond filling.

## 8 ✒

# ADAPTED FROM ITALIAN FIFTEENTH-
# TO SIXTEENTH-CENTURY BROCADE

This lovely design is from a table covering in a fine Renaissance painting.

OUTLINE: upper light color curve (lower light color curve is part of fill)
STITCH LENGTH: outline—covering 4 threads
                    fill—covering 2* and 4 threads
STEPS: up or down 2 threads
COLORS: 2. See color page 67.

* The upper right corner of the photograph locates the stitches covering 2 threads.

A. Start from the center of the canvas, count to the right 12 holes.
B. Make the outline of an upper curve (arrow):

| 1. Asc. lt. 3 singles | 2. Desc. lt. 2 triples |
|---|---|
| 1 double | 1 double |
| 3 triples | 3 singles |
| (top of curve) | skip a stitch |
| | (or 4th single) |

C. Repeat B across the canvas, then from the 1st stitch asc. and desc. right, etc.
D. Make outline row above:
    In the previous outline, from the 1st or 3rd stitch at the top of any curve, count up 2 holes. Repeat B and C.
E. Make outline row below:
    In the original outline, from any skipped stitch, count down 2 holes, make a triple stitch. Repeat B2, B1 and 2, C.
F. Cover the canvas with outlines.
G. Carry on and complete.

# 9 ✍

## ADAPTED FROM FRENCH
## NINETEENTH-CENTURY FABRIC,
## TOILE COLBERT

This impressive nineteenth-century design was based on an eighteenth-century pattern, although in the color photograph it looks Navaho.

Turn the book around so that the stitches in the photograph are vertical.

OUTLINE: large and small motif

STITCH LENGTH: covering 4 threads

STEPS: up or down 2 threads

COLORS: 2. 4 grad. of 1st color; 3 grad. of 2nd color. See color page 68.

A. Start from the center of the canvas, count up 4 holes.
B. Make the outline of a small motif (arrow):
   Each diagonal is 4 stitches, then change direction, etc.
C. Surround the small motif with 4 large motifs:
   To mark the distance between the small and large motifs:
   Vertically: Insert 4 sts. (temporary).
   Horizontally: Insert 8 sts. (temporary), skip 9th stitch.
   Large motif: each diagonal is 5 stitches, then change direction, etc.
D. Surround the large motifs with small motifs, etc.
E. Carry on and complete.

# 10 ✍

# ADAPTED FROM CENTRAL ASIAN (TURKOMAN) EIGHTEENTH-CENTURY BESHIR RUG

This design, worked in eighteenth-century colors, is very beautiful.

OUTLINE: twin peak diamonds

STITCH LENGTH: covering 4 threads

STEPS: up or down 2 threads

COLORS: 2 or 3. 3 grad. of 1st color; 3 grad. of 2nd color, or use 2 grad. of 2nd color plus white. See color page 67.

A. Start at the center of the canvas.

B. Make the outline of a twin peak diamond (arrow):
   Long sides: Asc. and desc. 10 sts. *each side.*
   Short sides: Asc. and desc. 5 sts. *each side.*
   Repeat to the left and then right across the canvas.

C. Make outline rows above and below:
   The rows of outline twin peak diamonds are separated by 3 holes between their vertical points.

D. Cover the canvas with outlines.

E. Carry on and complete.

NOTE: You have automatically outlined the row of alternating large and small diamonds by repeating the row of twin peak diamond motifs.
   The left side of the photograph shows how to alternate the color and the design within the twin peak diamonds, both horizontally and vertically.

# 11 ✍

## INSPIRED BY TURKISH (ERZURUM) THIRTEENTH-CENTURY SELJUK BRICKWORK

This beautiful design dates from 1253 and was used in the decoration of a religious school, under the patronage of Huand Hatun, the daughter of a Seljuk prince. (See photo page 140.)

OUTLINE: motif with 3 parts
STITCH LENGTH: covering 4 threads
STEPS: up or down 2 threads
COLORS: 3. For a three-dimensional effect  a. top—light color
                                                b. left—dark
                                                c. right—bright

See color page 69.

A. Start from the center of the canvas, count up 4 holes.
B. Make the outline of a 3 part motif (arrow):

| | | | | | |
|---|---|---|---|---|---|
| 1. Asc. lt. | 6 | dbl. sts. light | 8. Asc. vert. | 3 | dbl. sts. bright |
| 2. Desc. lt. | 2 | dbl. sts. light | 9. Asc. rt. | 4 | dbl. sts. bright |
| 3. Desc. vert. | 4 | dbl. sts. dark | 10. Asc. vert. | 1 | dbl. st. bright |
| 4. Desc. rt. | 5 | dbl. sts. dark | 11. Asc. lt. | 2 | dbl. sts. bright |
| 5. Desc. vert. | 2 | dbl. sts. dark | Change color and continue | | |
| 6. Desc. rt. | 3½ | dbl. sts. dark | Asc. lt. | 3 | dbl. sts. light |
| 7. Asc. rt. | 4½ | dbl. sts. bright | 12. Desc. lt. | 4 | dbl. sts. light |

C. To build the design vertically—the bottom of one motif fits into the top of the adjoining motif.
D. To build the design diagonally—the dark part of one motif is next to the bright part of the adjoining motif.
E. Cover the canvas with outlines and carry on.

NOTE: The sides of the outline are all asymmetrical, so watch the count carefully, otherwise the motifs will not fit into one another.

# 12 ✒

# INSPIRED BY FRENCH
# SIXTEENTH-CENTURY BROCADE

This elegant design graced a beautiful piece of French furniture.

Turn the book around so that the stitches in the photograph are vertical.

OUTLINE: zigzag lines and flowers

STITCH LENGTH: covering 2 and 4 threads

STEPS: up or down 2 threads

COLORS: 2. 4 grad. of 1st color (use the lightest grade for the background); 2 grad. of 2nd color. See color page 70.

A. Start in the center of the canvas.

B. Make a zigzag line (arrow):
   Asc. and desc. 9 dbl. sts. Repeat to the left and then right, across the canvas.

C. Make flowers across the canvas:
   From every vertical point in the previous zigzag line, insert 1 dbl. st. (temporary). Then start the base of each flower, etc., turn the canvas upside down when necessary.

D. Make a new zigzag line above and below the flowers:
   From the top of each flower, insert 3 dbl. sts. (temporary).
   Then start one of the top points of the new zigzag line. Follow B.

E. Cover the canvas with zigzag lines and flowers. Carry on.
   Note the direction of the flowers.

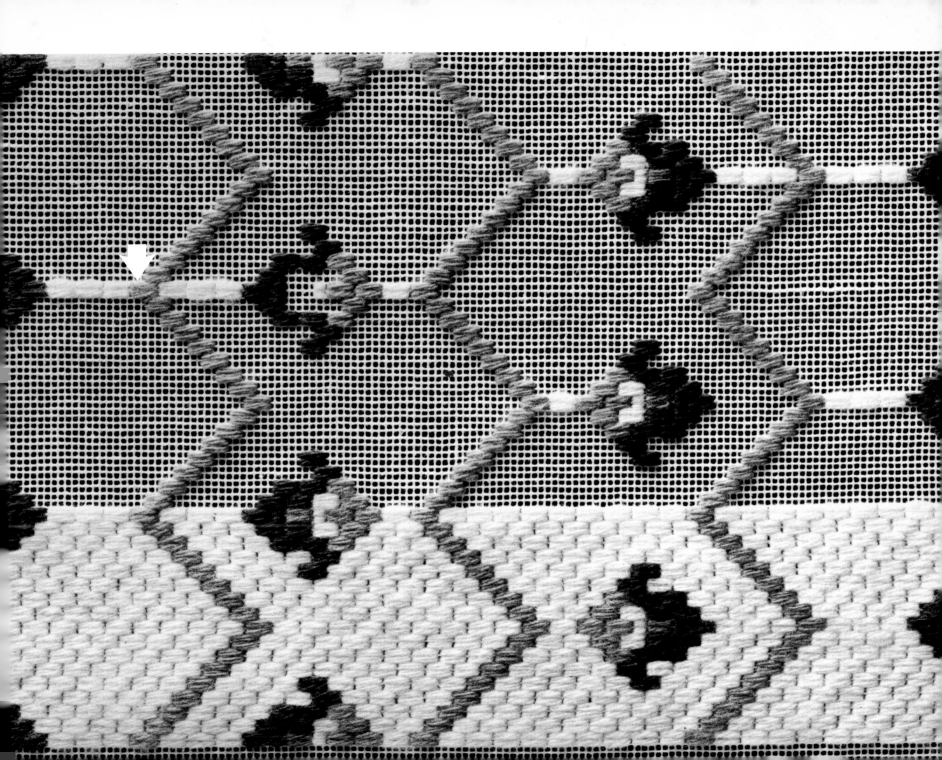

## 13

# INSPIRED BY EGYPTIAN (MAMELUKE)
# SIXTEENTH-CENTURY DECORATED PAGE
# OF THE KORAN

The Mamelukes rose from slavery to rule Egypt for three centuries and created such powerful things as this design.

OUTLINE: large diamond motif cluster, comprising interior and exterior small diamonds

STITCH LENGTH: covering 4 threads

STEPS: up or down 2 threads

COLORS: 2. 4 grad. of each color, using a grade of one for the background. See color page 77.

SPECIAL PROJECTS: upholstery for a piano bench

A. Start from the center of the canvas, count to the right 16 holes.

B. Make the outline of a large diamond (arrow):
   Asc. and desc. 17 sts. *each side*.

C. Make the outline of the small interior diamonds:
   From the horizontal point (arrow) of the large diamond, count to its 8th stitch.
   Work toward the center of the large diamond.
   Asc. or desc. 8 sts. *each side*.

D. Make the outline of the small exterior diamonds:
   Work away from the horizontal point of the large diamond.
   Asc. and desc. 8 sts. *each side*.

E. To mark the distance between each large diamond motif cluster:
   Horizontally—insert 3 sts. (temporary).
   Vertically—insert 5 sts. (temporary) if you wish to make more motifs in this direction.

F. Cover the canvas with outlines and carry on.

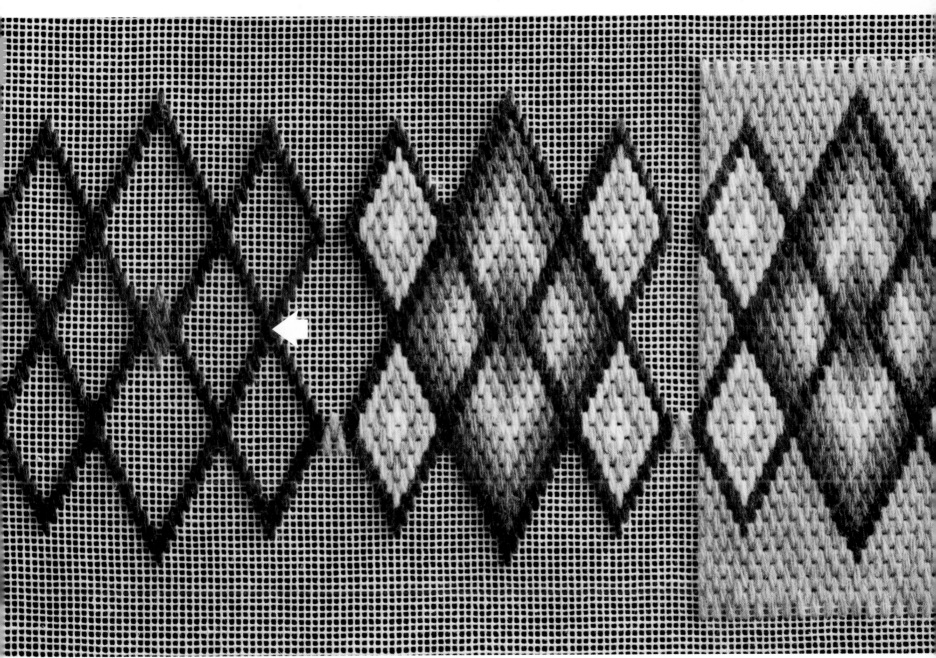

# 14 🖋

# ADAPTED FROM AMERICAN EIGHTEENTH-CENTURY QUILT

This strong design originally dates back to 1776 and was called "New York Beauty."

OUTLINE: diamond centers and diagonal lines
STITCH LENGTH: covering 4 threads
STEPS: up or down 2 threads
COLORS: 4. The diamond centers are the same color as the background. For the diagonals connecting the diamonds, use 2 colors in each pair of stitches. They should be the same color as the two outer rows of the diamonds. See color page 69.

A. Start from the center of the canvas, count up 2 holes.
B. Make a small diamond center (arrow):
    Asc. and desc. 3 dbl. sts. *each side*.
C. Next to the middle stitches of the diamond center make diagonal lines going out in four directions. 11 dbl. sts. each line.
D. Make new diamond centers (at the ends of these diagonals). Follow B.
E. Repeat B, C and D until the canvas is covered.
F. Surround each diamond center with 3 more rows.
G. Make the background.

# 15 ✒

# ADAPTED FROM ITALIAN
# NINETEENTH-CENTURY LACE

This delightful design is from a piece of Buratto lace, of the Abruzzi, which is now in the Metropolitan Museum of Art, New York. (See photo page 142.)

OUTLINE: plateaus (flat top mountains ⌐⌐ ) and floral motifs
STITCH LENGTH: covering 4 threads
STEPS: up or down 2 threads
COLORS: 4. 2 grad. each of 3 colors plus the background color. See color
      page 76.

A. Start at the center of the canvas.
B. Make the outline of the plateaus (arrow). Insert 1st stitch then,
    Asc. 9 sts.
    Horiz. line 12 sts. (Alternate 1 st. down, next up, etc.)
    Desc. 9 sts. Repeat to the left, and then right across the canvas.
C. Make the floral motifs below the plateaus (B) across the canvas:
    The top of the flower is 4 holes from the middle stitch of the horizontal line in every plateau.
    The bottom of the flower stem is 4 holes from the lowest point of every plateau.
D. Continue making alternate rows of plateaus and floral motifs above and below.
E. Above each plateau outline row, add 2 rows.
    The 2nd row (medium dark) requires careful attention.
    The bottom left of the photograph shows the 2nd row before being filled in.
F. Make the background.

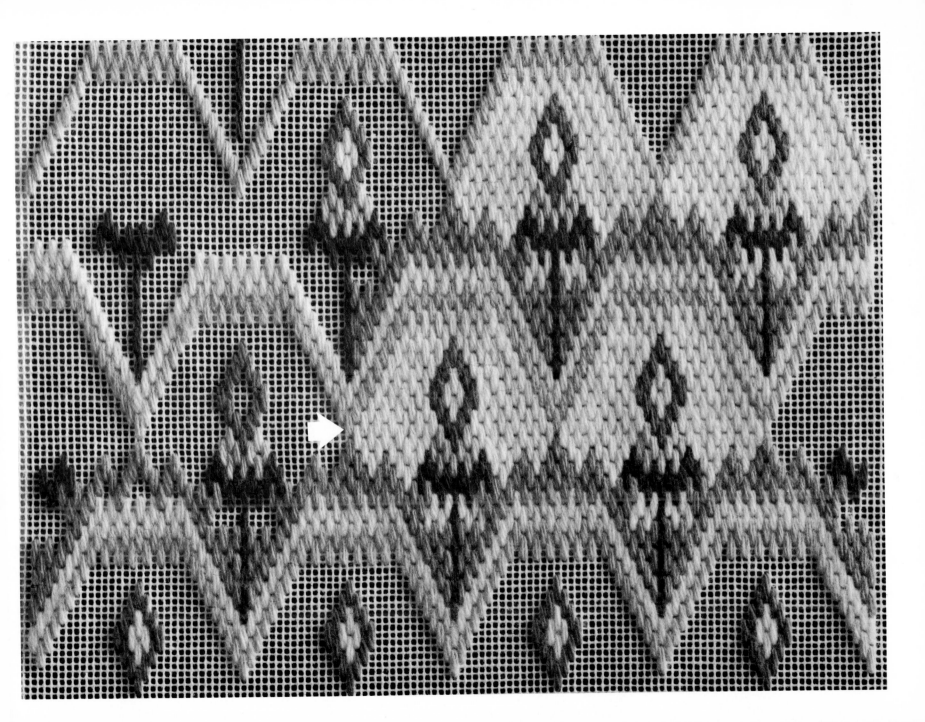

# 16 ✍

# INSPIRED BY SONIA DELAUNEY
# DESIGN, CIRCA 1930 (ART DECO)

This gifted painter inspired a most original treatment of these shapes.

OUTLINE: small diamonds, squared-off areas around (or behind) the diamonds, and vertical lines

STITCH LENGTH: covering 2 and 4 threads

STEPS: up or down 2 threads

COLORS: 4. See color page 78.

A. Start at the center of the canvas.

B. Make the outline of a small diamond (arrow):
   Asc. and desc. 5 sts. *each side*.
   Make a vertical row of diamonds all in the same color.
   To the right and left of this row attach small diamonds in another color, also in vertical rows. Making 3 vertical rows altogether of attached diamonds, the length of the canvas.
   Work to either the right or left of the diamonds in the following order (complete each stage the length of the canvas).

C. Squared off area around the small diamonds:
   The horizontal effect is achieved by alternating stitches covering 2 and 4 threads. Check the upper left of the photograph.

D. Work 4 vertical lines, each line is 2 stitches wide.

E. Same as C in reverse.

F. Same as B. Repeat. Carry on.

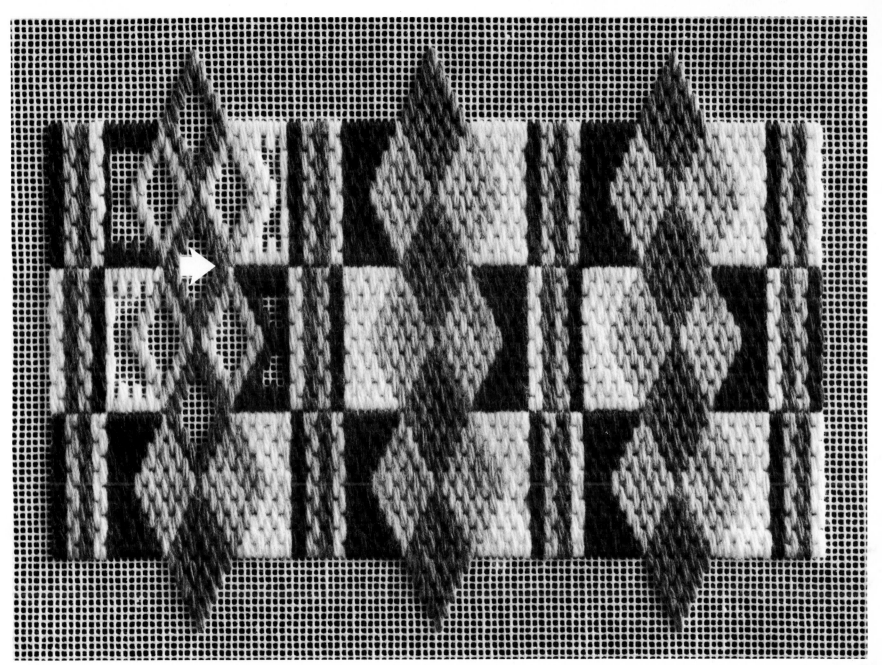

# 17 ✍

# INSPIRED BY ARABIC
# NINTH-CENTURY EMBROIDERY

During the Golden Age of the Arabian Empire they created such sophisticated designs as this one.

OUTLINE: large and small diamonds
STITCH LENGTH: covering 4 threads
STEPS: up or down 2 threads
COLORS: 4. See color page 79.

A. Start from the center of the canvas, count to the right 13 holes.
B. Make the outline of a large diamond (arrow):
  Asc. and desc. 14 sts. *each side.*
C. Cover the canvas with the outlines of these diamonds.
D. At the 4 points of every large diamond, make small diamonds.
  Asc. and desc. 9 sts. *each side.*

  NOTE: The 5th stitch on each side of the small diamond was created by the large diamond intersecting it.

E. Fill in all remaining areas as shown.

# 18 ✍

## ADAPTED FROM GERMAN
## SIXTEENTH-CENTURY ORNAMENT BOOK

This design and the following one are based on the same source. By broadening the diamond and working the background all in one color, a placid effect is achieved.

OUTLINE: interlocking diamonds
STITCH LENGTH: covering 4 threads
STEPS: up or down 2 threads
COLORS: 2. 2 grad. of 1st color (use one grade for the background); 1 grade of 2nd color. See color page 76.

A. Start from the center of the canvas, count up 20 holes.
B. Make a diamond (arrow):
   Asc. and desc. 12 dbl. sts. *each side*.
   In making the diamond always work counterclockwise and skip the 4th double stitch on each side of the diamond.
C. To interlock the diamonds, horizontally and vertically.
   In the skipped spaces of the previous diamond, start in the other color, and make 4 dbl. sts.; change direction (work again counterclockwise). Follow B. Repeat.
D. Cover the canvas with interlocking diamonds. Complete.

# 19 ✍

## ADAPTED FROM GERMAN
## SIXTEENTH-CENTURY ORNAMENT BOOK

This design and the previous one are based on the same source. By elongating the diamond and working the background in 2 colors, an active effect is achieved.

OUTLINE: interlocking diamonds
STITCH LENGTH: covering 4 threads
STEPS: up or down 2 threads
COLORS: 4. See color page 72.

A. Start from the center of the canvas, count up 26 holes.
B. Make a diamond (arrow):
   Asc. and desc. 15 dbl. sts. *each side*.
   In making the diamond always work counterclockwise and skip the 5th double stitch on each side of the diamond.
C. To interlock the diamonds, horizontally and vertically:
   In skipped spaces of the previous diamond, start in the other color and make 5 dbl. sts., change direction (again, work counterclockwise). Follow B. Repeat.
D. Cover the canvas with interlocking diamonds. Complete.

## 20 ✒

# ADAPTED FROM GREEK
# EIGHTEENTH-CENTURY RUG

This gorgeous design is great fun to make.

OUTLINE: 5 large diamond motif—consisting of a full (fully shown) diamond with a light center plus its pairs of side diamonds

STITCH LENGTH: covering 4 threads

STEPS: up or down 2 threads

COLORS: 5. 2 grad. each of 1st and 2nd colors; 3 grad. each of 3rd and 4th colors; 4 grad. of 5th color. See color page 75.

A. Start from the center of the canvas, count to the right 14 holes.

B. Make the outline of a full diamond (arrow):
   Asc. and desc. 15 sts. *each side.*

C. Make two side diamonds on either side of the full diamond.

D. Work in a mirror image, the five large diamond motif. Repeat these across the canvas.

E. Make the outline of the five large diamond motif above and below:
   From the vertical points of the full diamond, make the next row following B–D.

F. When the canvas is covered with outlines, fill in the remaining areas as shown.

NOTE: You have automatically outlined the row of small and twin-filled diamonds by repeating the row of five large diamond motifs.

## 21 ⚞

# ADAPTED FROM BELGIUM (TONGRES) FOURTEENTH-CENTURY EMBROIDERED ALMS PURSE

This handsome design was originally used on an alms purse that belongs to the Church of Notre Dame de Tongres, Belgium.

OUTLINE: large interlocking diamonds
STITCH LENGTH: outline—covering 4 threads
                     fill—covering 2* and 4 threads
STEPS: up or down 2 threads
COLORS: 7. See color page 76.

* The lower left of the photograph shows the location of all stitches covering 2 threads.

A. Start from the center of the canvas, count up 4 holes.
B. Make the outline of a large diamond (arrow):
     Asc. and desc. 14 dbl. sts. *each side*.
C. To interlock the diamonds, horizontally and vertically:
     From all the points of the previous diamond, count to the 4th stitch and working toward its center, make 3 dbl. sts., change direction. Follow B.
D. When the canvas is covered with interlocked diamonds, fill.
     The horizontal line at the top and bottom edge of the squares is achieved by alternating double stitches covering 2 and 4 threads.

CHECK PHOTOGRAPH: The motifs within the squares alternate both horizontally and vertically.

## 22 ✒

# INSPIRED BY FORMOSA
# (ABORIGINE) FABRIC

This interesting design was created on East Coast Atayal (Formosa), ramie cloth.

OUTLINE: diamond (whose horizontal point is indicated by the arrow)
STITCH LENGTH: covering 4 threads
STEPS: up or down 2 threads
COLORS: 2. 3 grad. of 1st color, 4 grad. of 2nd color. See color page 77.

A. Start from the center of the canvas, count to the right 2 holes.
B. Make the outline of a diamond (arrow):
   Asc. and desc. 16 sts. *each side*.
C. To make the adjoining diamonds, horizontally and vertically:
   From all the points of the previous diamond, count to the 3rd stitch and working toward its center make 2 stitches. Change direction, then follow B.
D. Cover the canvas with the diamond outlines. Carry on.
CHECK PHOTOGRAPH: The patterns within the diamonds alternate horizontally as well as in every other row.

55

## 23 🖎

# ADAPTED FROM EGYPTIAN
# VTH DYNASTY PAINTED PANEL

This fine and very early design is from the tomb of Ptah-hetep. The dates of the Vth Dynasty are 2494–2345 B.C.

OUTLINE: small blocks and diamonds
STITCH LENGTH: covering 2 and 4 threads
STEPS: up or down 2 threads
COLORS: 2. 4 grad. of 1st color plus a contrasting color. See color page 66.

A. Start from the center of the canvas, count up 24 holes.
   This is the center (or 3rd) stitch of a block.
B. Make block (arrow):
   1st, 3rd and 5th sts. are long (cover 4).
   2nd and 4th sts. are each made up of 2 short stitches (cover 2), one on top of the other.
C. Make the outline of the top half of a diamond. Under the 2nd or 4th stitch of a block make:
   1st st. short.
   Asc. or desc. 10 long sts.
   11th st. short.
D. Make another block, following B.
E. Repeat C and B to the left, and then right across the canvas.
F. Turn the canvas upside down, make the bottom half of the diamonds and blocks across canvas.
G. Cover the canvas with diamond outlines, blocks and complete.

## 24 🖎

# ADAPTED FROM ENGLISH
# EIGHTEENTH-CENTURY QUILT

This charming design embodies the love of curves in the mid-eighteenth century.

OUTLINE: high and low curves
STITCH LENGTH: outline—covering 4 threads
                   fill—covering 2* and 4 threads
STEPS: up or down 2 threads
COLORS: 6. See color page 70.

* The left side of the photograph shows the location of all stitches covering 2 threads.

A. Start at the mid-point of the bottom edge of the canvas.
B. Make the outline of a low and high curve (arrow). Insert 1st stitch,

| | | | | |
|---|---|---|---|---|
| 1. Asc. lt. | 1 single | | 4. Desc. lt. | 1 triple |
| | 1 double | | | 1 double |
| | 1 triple | | | 3 singles |
| | 1 quadruple (top of low curve) | | | 1 double |
| 2. Desc. lt. | 1 triple | | 5. Asc. lt. | 1 triple |
| | 1 double | | | 1 quadruple (top of low curve) |
| 3. Asc. lt. | 3 singles | | 6. Desc. lt. | 1 triple |
| | 1 double | | | 1 double |
| | 1 triple | | | 2 singles |
| | 1 quintuple (top of high curve) | | | |

Repeat these across the canvas. Asc. and desc. to the right of the 1st stitch.
C. Make the outline rows above: Directly above the middle stitch at the top of any high curve, in the previous row, start 1st stitch. Follow B.
D. When the canvas is covered with outlines, fill.

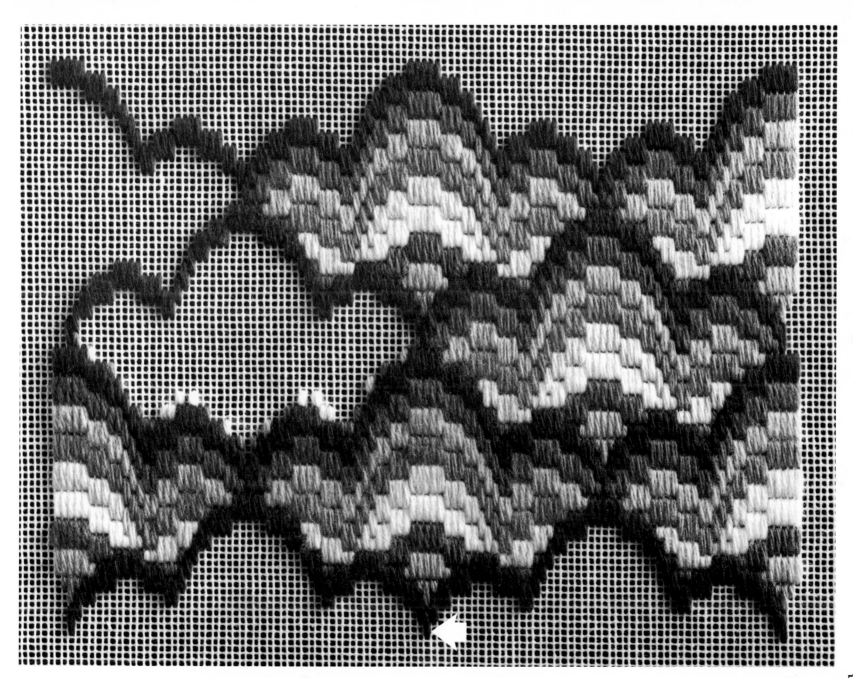

## 25 ✍

## INSPIRED BY BYZANTINE
## MOSAIC, CIRCA 547 A.D.

This classic design is on mosaics in the Church of San Vitale, Ravenna, Italy.

OUTLINE: largest curves
STITCH LENGTH: outline—covering 4 threads
                fill—covering 2* and 4 threads
STEPS: up or down 2 threads
COLORS: 3. 3 grad. each of 1st and 2nd colors; 1 grade of 3rd color for outline. See color page 77.

* The top of the left side of the photograph shows the location of all stitches covering 2 threads.

A. Start at the mid-point of the bottom edge of the canvas.
B. Make the outline of a curve (arrow). Insert 1st stitch, then:

| 1. Asc. lt. 7 singles | 2. Desc. lt. 1 quadruple |
|---|---|
| 1 double | 1 triple |
| 1 triple | 1 double |
| 1 quadruple | 8 singles |
| 1 quintuple (top of curve) | |

Repeat these across the canvas. Asc. and desc. to the right of the 1st stitch.
C. Make the outline rows above: Directly above the middle stitch at the top of any curve, in the previous row, start 1st stitch. Follow B.
D. Cover the canvas with outlines and complete.

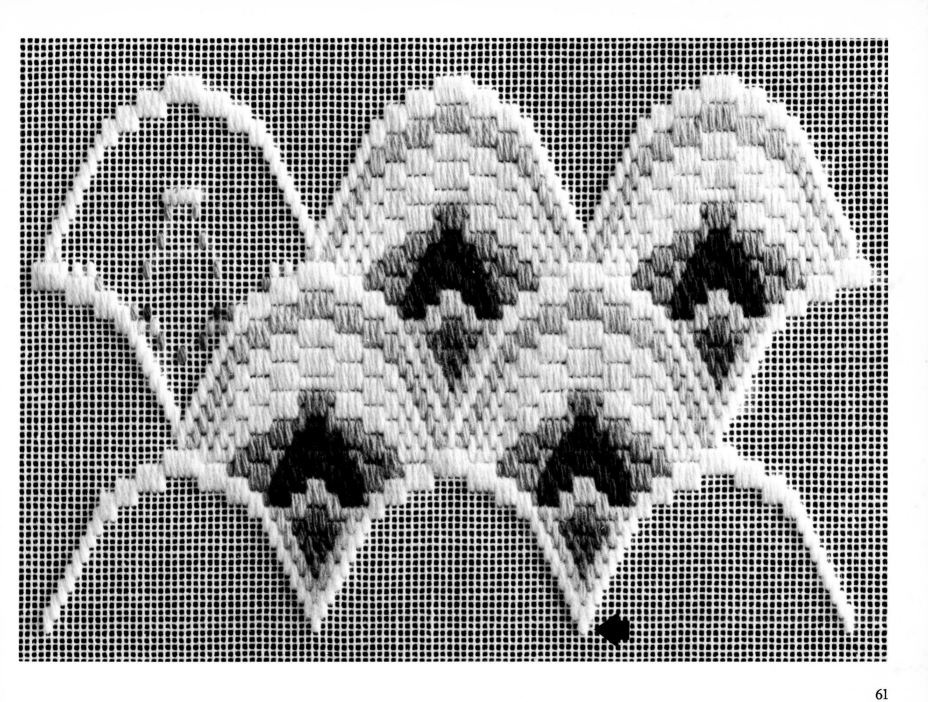

## 26 ✍

# ADAPTED FROM DANISH SAMPLER, CIRCA 1751

The sampler from which this handsome design comes is in the Victoria and Albert Museum, London.

OUTLINE: triple zigzag motif (lower left photograph)
STITCH LENGTH: covering 4 threads
STEPS: up or down 2 threads
COLORS: 6. See color page 77.

A. Start from the center of the canvas, count up 18 holes.

B. Make the outline of a triple zigzag motif (arrow). Insert 1st double stitch, then:

| | |
|---|---|
| 1. Desc. lt. 3 dbl. sts. | 6. Desc. rt. 3 dbl. sts. |
| 2. Asc. lt. 3 dbl. sts. | 7. Desc. lt. 3 dbl. sts. |
| 3. Desc. lt. 4 dbl. sts. | 8. Desc. rt. 4 dbl. sts. |
| 4. Desc. rt. 3 dbl. sts. | 9. Asc. rt. 3 dbl. sts. |
| 5. Desc. lt. 3 dbl. sts. | 10. Desc. rt. 3 dbl. sts. |

Turn the canvas upside down. Repeat 1–10.

C. Use each 4-stitch diagonal end (see indicator) as a start of a new triple zigzag motif. Cover the canvas with them. In this way you will automatically create the outline of the double zigzag motif.

D. Fill in the remaining areas as shown.

## 27 ✍

# ADAPTED FROM AMERICAN QUILT, CIRCA 1830

This engaging design is from a quilt in the Collection of the Shelburne Museum, Shelburne, Vermont.

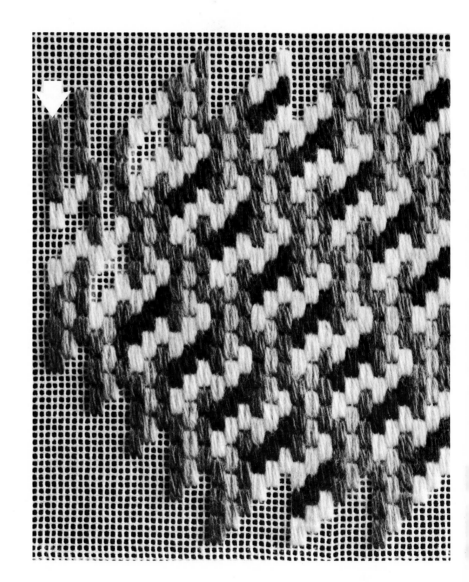

OUTLINE: 2 pairs of 3 vertical stitches and
         2 pairs of 3 diagonal stitches (see arrow)
STITCH LENGTH: covering 4 threads
STEPS: up or down 2 threads
COLORS: 4. See color page 68.

A. Start at the top, left edge of the canvas.
B. Make the 1st pair of 3 vertical stitches (arrow):
    These pairs go diagonally from the upper left to the lower right of
    the canvas; treat the middle row as fill.
C. Make pairs of diagonal stitches directly above and below vertical
    stitches. These too will form a diagonal pattern going from the upper left to the lower right. Again, treat the middle row as fill.
D. Cover the canvas with these pairs, then fill.

NOTE: For clarity, the fill within each pair has been left out in the upper
    left of the photograph. The fill colors add extra contrasts.

54

52

55

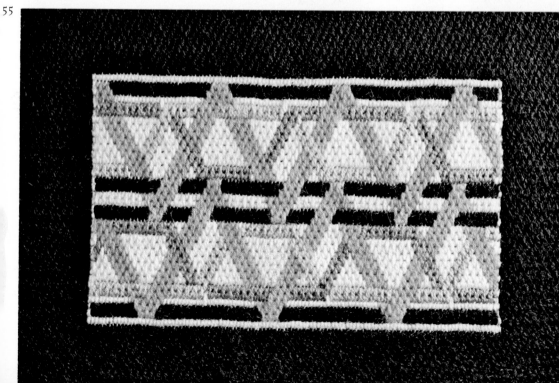

*For instruction in working these patterns,
see corresponding black and white design numbers.*

65

31

50

43

66

23

8

39

2

10

60

27

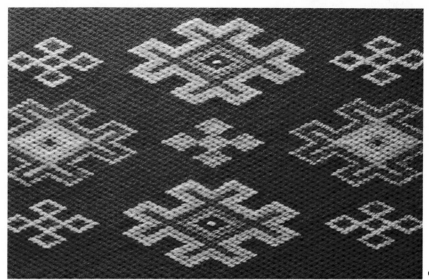

9

4

7

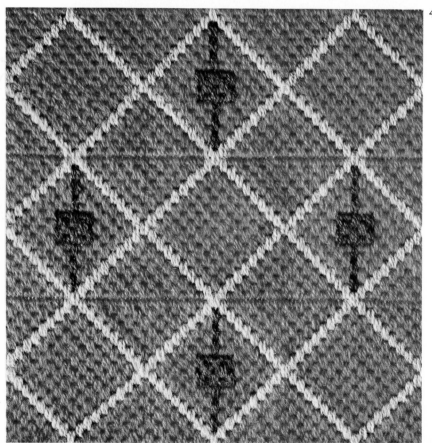

68

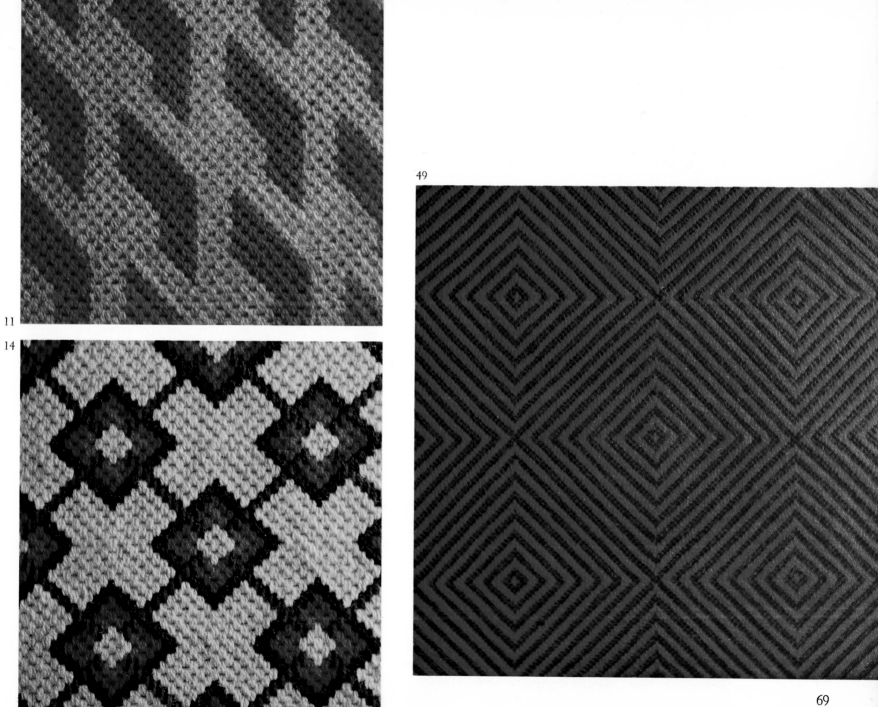

11

14

49

42

1

53

71

45

72

6

38

19

33    34              37              35              36

73

74

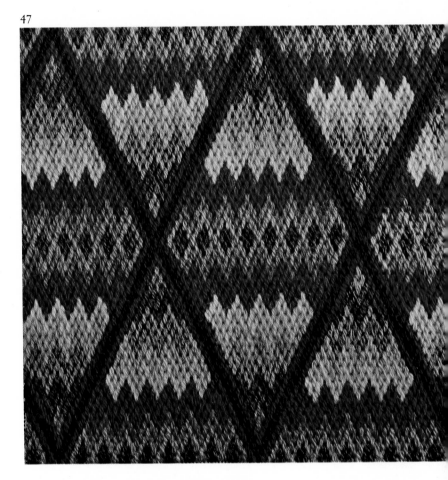

56

47

20

40

48

75

15

44

21

18

76

25

22

26

13

5

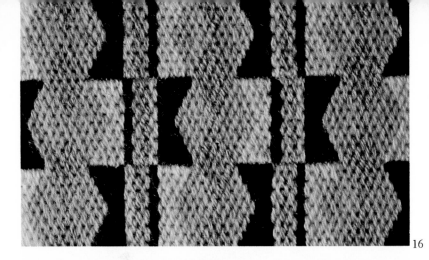

16

59

51

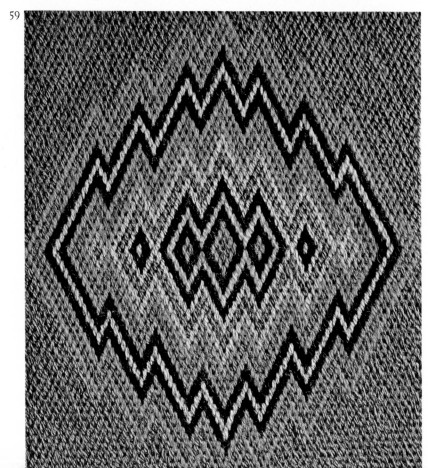

78

28

3

17

61

79

62

5"

46

58

## 28 ✒

# ADAPTED FROM AMERICAN
# MID-NINETEENTH-CENTURY QUILT

This amusing design was called "Baby Blocks" in the last century.

OUTLINE: top of box—covering 2, 4 and 6 threads
               bottom of box—covering 6 threads

STEPS: top of box—up or down 3 and 5 threads
         bottom of box—up or down 5 threads

NOTE: Each stitch in the entire design is either one hole above or below
the stitch next to it.

COLORS: 3. See color page 79.
         For a three-dimensional effect make top section box—medium-
bright color; lower left section—light; lower right section—dark

A. Start from the mid-point at the top edge of the canvas.
B. Make the dark, lower right, section of a box (arrow):
     4 desc. sts.

     NOTE: To start next section of 4 desc. sts., step up, to left, 1 thread.
         Work these dark sections in a diagonal line.

C. Make the light, lower left, section:
     3 desc. sts.
     Start first light section by attaching it to a dark section.
     Work these light sections in a diagonal line.
D. Keep building, till dark and light sections are all attached and cover
the canvas.
E. Finally, fill in the top section—covering 2, 4, 6, 4 and 2 threads.

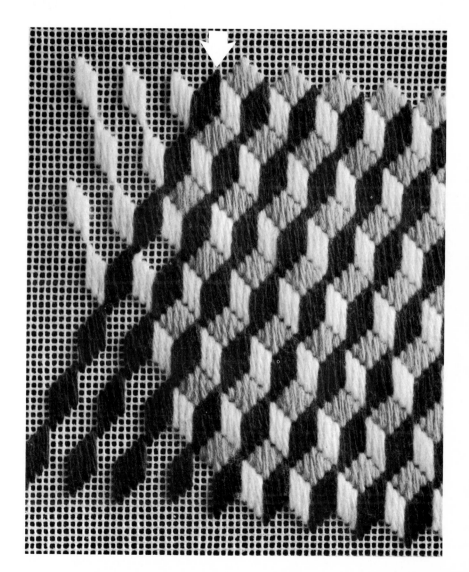

## 29 ✍

# ADAPTED FROM AMERICAN FABRIC, DOUBLE WEAVE, CIRCA 1805

This sweet design is from a coverlet in the Museum of Science and Industry, Chicago.

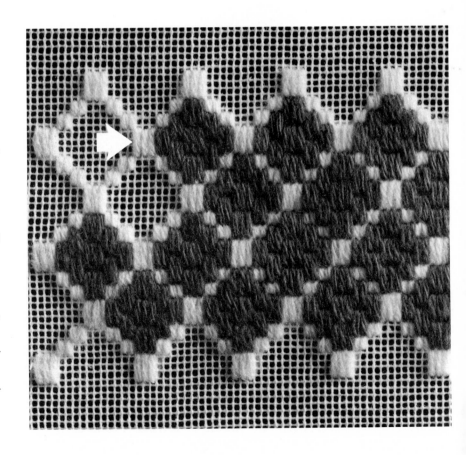

OUTLINE: diamonds

STITCH LENGTH: covering 2 (doubles) and 4 (triples) threads

STEPS: up or down 0 threads

    NOTE: Stitches are above (on a diagonal) not next to each other.

COLORS: 2. See color page 70.

SPECIAL PROJECTS: frame (photo or mirror)

A. Start from the center of the canvas, count to the right 6 holes.

B. Make the outline of the top half of a diamond (arrow). Insert 1st triple stitch, then:

    1. Asc. lt. 2 doubles    2. Desc. lt. 2 doubles

          1 triple               1 triple

    Repeat these across the canvas, then from the 1st triple stitch, asc. and desc. right.

C. Turn the canvas upside down and make the bottom half of the diamond.

D. Follow guide B and C, covering the canvas above and below with diamond outlines.

E. Fill in the diamonds as shown.

## 30 ✍

# ADAPTED FROM EGYPTIAN
# VTH DYNASTY PAINTED PANEL

This exciting and very ancient design is from the tomb of Ptah-hetep.
The Vth Dynasty dates 2494–2345 B.C.

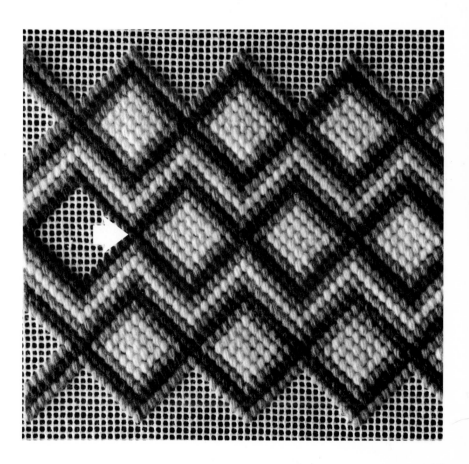

OUTLINE: dark diamonds

STITCH LENGTH: covering 2 threads

STEPS: up or down 1 thread

COLORS: 3. Dark, medium dark and bright. For a lively effect always surround a bright with a medium-dark color. See color page 70.

SPECIAL PROJECTS: wallets, eyeglass case, slippers, boxes

A. Start from the center of the canvas, count to the right 8 holes.

B. Make the outline of a diamond (arrow):
    Asc. and desc. 9 sts. *each side*.

C. Repeat these to the left, and then right across the canvas.

D. Add 3 rows above and below.

E. Repeat the diamond outline, then rows, etc.

F. Fill in the diamonds as shown.

# 31

## ADAPTED FROM GERMAN
## EARLY-NINETEENTH-CENTURY BROCADE

This charming design is from the Collection of the Austrian Museum for Art and Industry.

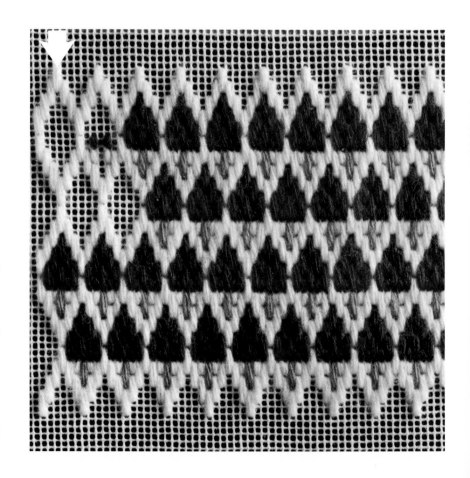

OUTLINE: zigzag rows
STITCH LENGTH: outline—covering 4 threads
                     fill—covering 2* and 4 threads
STEPS: up or down 2 threads
COLORS: 3. See color page 66.
SPECIAL PROJECTS: slippers, picture frame, checkbook cover

A. Start in the center of the canvas.
B. Make a zigzag row (arrow):
    Asc. and desc. 4 sts. Repeat to the left, and then right across the canvas.
C. Turn the canvas upside down. Repeat B.

    NOTE: The 1st stitch in the new row is directly under any lowest stitch of the previous row.

D. Cover the canvas above and below with zigzag outlines.
E. Fill as shown.

* The upper left corner of the photograph shows the location of all stitches covering 2 threads.

# 32 ✍

## ADAPTED FROM NEW ZEALAND (MAORI) INTERWOVEN REEDS

This exciting design is on a wall panel from a meeting house, presently in the Hamburg Museum fur Volkerkunste und Vorgeschichte.

OUTLINE: 2 rows of diamonds, one divided by the horiz. edges of the panels

> NOTE: If this design is repeated horizontally the effect is not of panels but of broad horizontal stripes.

STITCH LENGTH: covering 2 and 4 threads
STEPS: up or down 2 threads
COLORS: 4. See color page 70. For the greatest effect, follow the color placement carefully.
SPECIAL PROJECTS: borders of desk blotter, straps for luggage rack

A. Start from the center of the canvas, count to the right 6 holes.
B. Make the outline of a divided diamond (arrow):
   1. Horiz. pt. is 1 short st. (covering 2).
   2. Asc. 6 sts.
   3. Desc. 5 sts. Repeat across canvas.
C. Turn the canvas upside down and repeat B in the other color.
D. Make the inner row and fill.
E. Make the outline of a complete diamond.
   Asc. and desc. 7 sts. *each side*. Repeat these across the canvas. Make the inner row and fill.
F. Repeat B–E till the canvas is covered.

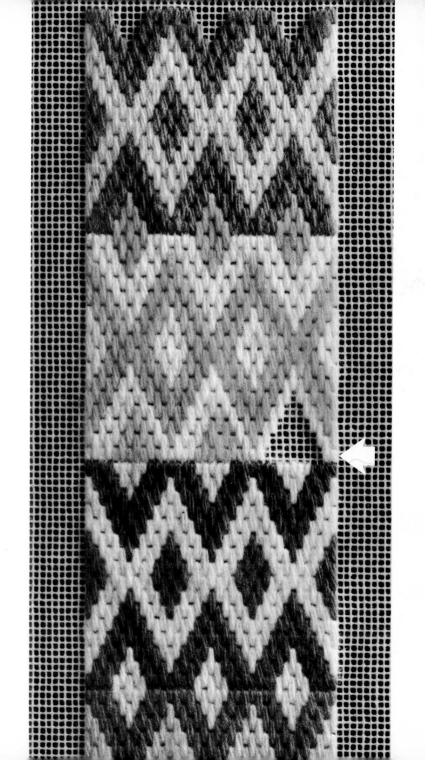

## 33 ✍

# ADAPTED FROM ITALIAN EIGHTEENTH-CENTURY CUT-VELVET BORDER

This fine design is to be found in the Museo V. Ferrari, Milan.

OUTLINE: small hexagons and diamonds

STITCH LENGTH: small hexagonal and diamond outlines—covering
        2 threads
        diamond fill—covering 2, 3 and 4 threads*
        small hexagonal fill—2, 4 and 6 threads
        edge fill—covering 1 thru 6 threads

STEPS: up or down 1 thru 5 threads

COLORS: 3. See color page 73.

SPECIAL PROJECTS: hatbands, belts, borders

* The right side of the photograph clarifies the stitch length of the diamond fill.

A. Start from the center of the canvas, count up 5 holes.

B. Make the outline of a small hexagon (arrow):
        Diagonals: 7 sts. *each side.*
        Horizontals: 9 sts. across.
        Create these small hexagons across the canvas.

C. Fill in all remaining areas as shown.

VARIATIONS: 1. For a narrower design—make only 1 line of small hexagons and use the edge fill on both sides of these hexagons.

2. To border the design—make a border on each side, covering 3 threads.

3. For a wider design (vertically)—use the diamond fill, instead of the edge fill, at the sides of the small hexagons.

## 34 ✍

# ADAPTED FROM JAPANESE
# TRADITIONAL SWORD HANGING

This nice design is made very quickly.

OUTLINE: diamonds and horizontal lines

STITCH LENGTH:   1. Diamond outline—covering 4 threads
2. Horizontal line—covering 2 threads
3. Background fill—covering 4 threads
4. Background meets horizontal line—stitches covering 3 alternate with 5.*
5. Outer edge—stitches covering 2 alternate with 4.*

STEPS: up and down 2 threads, except where the horizontal point of the diamond meets the horizontal line—up or down 1 thread.

COLORS: 5. See color page 73.

A. Start from the center of the canvas, count to the right 8 holes.
B. Make the outline of a diamond (arrow):
   Asc. and desc. 9 sts. *each side*.
C. Make a horiz. line—9 sts.
D. Repeat B and C across the canvas to the left and then right. Complete.

\* The right bottom of the photograph shows no. 4 and no. 5 above.

## 35 ✍

## ADAPTED FROM ZAIRE, FORMERLY
## BELGIAN CONGO (BAMBALA SUBTRIBE)
## TEXTILE DESIGN

This elegant design is a traditional motif used on embroidered cloths and is presently in the British Museum, London.

OUTLINE: small, medium and interlocking pair of large diamonds, as well as 4 diagonal lines.

STITCH LENGTH: outline—covering 2 threads
　　　　　　　outline fill—covering 2, 4, 6, 8, 10 and 12 threads
　　　　　　　edge fill—covering 1 thru 11 threads
　　　　　　　border—covering 4 threads

STEPS: outline 　—up or down 1 thread
　　　outline fill—up or down 3, 5, 7, 9 and 11 threads
　　　edge fill 　—up or down 1 thru 9 threads
　　　border 　—up or down 4 threads

COLORS: 2. 2 grad. of 1st color; 2nd color contrasting. See color page 73.

A. Start from the center of the canvas, count to the right 20 holes.

B. Make a large diamond (arrow):
　　Asc. and desc. 13 sts. *each side.*

C. To interlock the next large diamond:
　　From the left horiz. pt. of the previous diamond count up 5 sts.
　　Working clockwise, desc. rt. 4 sts.; change direction, follow B.
　　Work in the following order:

D. Small diamonds (in the center of the large diamonds) asc. and desc. 5 sts. *each side.*

E. Medium diamonds—asc. and desc. 7 sts. *each side.*

F. 4 diagonal lines—6 sts. each line (extending from the vert. pts. of the medium diamond).

G. Repeat B–F to the left and then right across the canvas. Carry on and create this lovely satin effect.

# 36 ✍

# ADAPTED FROM ITALIAN EIGHTEENTH-CENTURY CUT VELVET BORDER

This elegant design is to be found in the Museo V. Ferrari, Milan.

OUTLINE: long diagonal lines and diamonds
STITCH LENGTH: outline—covering 2 threads
　　　　　　　　fill—covering 2 and 4 threads
STEPS: outline—up or down 0 threads

　　NOTE: The stitches are above (on a diagonal) not next to each other.

　　fill—up or down 2 threads
COLORS: 3. See color page 73.

A. Start from the mid-point of the bottom edge of the canvas.
B. Make a long diagonal line (arrow):
　　　Asc. rt. 12 dbl. sts.
C. Stitch across 1 row of 8 dbl. sts. to mark the distance to the next diagonal line.
D. Desc. left 12 dbl. sts. and continue as shown—this picture is worth a hundred words.

NOTE: At the horizontal points of the diamond, the double stitches repeat.

CHECK PHOTOGRAPH: when filling edge section for 3 vertical groups of 4 stitches each.

37 ✍

# INSPIRED BY ARABIC
# ELEVENTH-CENTURY TILE

This stunning design is presently in the Victoria and Albert Museum, London.

OUTLINE: hexagons, diamonds and background diamonds
STITCH LENGTH: outline—covering 2 threads
        fill    —covering 1, 3, 5, 6 and 7 threads
        border—covering 3 threads
STEPS: outline—up or down 2 threads
     fill    —up or down 2, 4, 5 and 6 threads
     border —up or down 3 threads
COLORS: 4, or 3 grad. of 1st color, second color contrasting. See color
       page 73.
SPECIAL PROJECTS: in monochromatic colors, makes a great belt for a man

A. Start from the center of the canvas, count to the right 9 holes.
B. Make the outline of a diamond (arrow):
    Asc. and desc. 10 sts. *each side*.
C. Make a hexagon—diagonals 10 sts. *each side*, horizontals 25 sts. across.
D. Cover the canvas to the left, and then right with these outlines.
E. Make the background diamonds (located between the hexagons and the diamonds):
    Asc. and desc. 5 sts. *each side*.

NOTE: In the background diamond, the stitch closest to the hexagon and the diamond covers 1 thread, the rest covers 2.

F. Fill as shown.

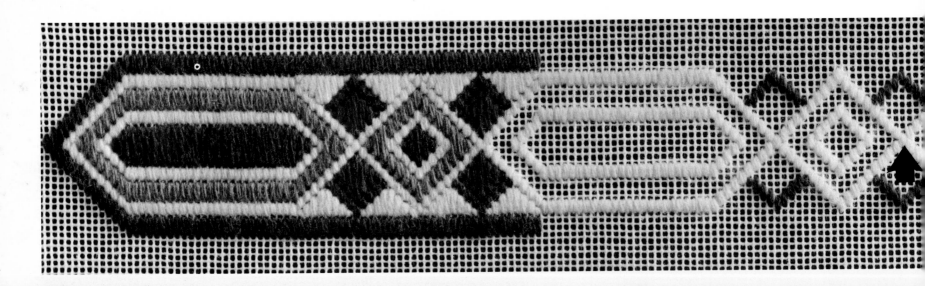

## 38 ✍

# ADAPTED FROM EGYPTIAN (COPTIC) EIGHTH-CENTURY TAPESTRY BORDER

This classic design has been used since antiquity.

OUTLINE: curves
STITCH LENGTH: covering 2* and 4 threads
STEPS: up or down 2 threads
COLORS: 3. 3 grad. each of 2 colors. 3rd color for the background. See color page 72.

A. Start from the mid-point of the left edge of the canvas, count up 8 holes.

B. Make the outline of a curve (arrow):

1. Asc.  rt. 1 double
    4 triples
    (last triple is
    top of curve)

2. Desc. rt. 3 triples
    2 doubles
    3 singles
    2 doubles
    4 triples
    (last triple is
    bottom of curve)

3. Asc.  rt. 3 triples (the last triple is made up of 2 sts. covering 4, the 3rd st. covers 2).

C. Start 2nd outline curve. See indicator.
    Repeat B and C across the canvas. Carry on and complete.

* The left half of the photograph shows the location of all stitches covering 2 threads.

# 39 ✍

# ADAPTED FROM JAPANESE
# TRADITIONAL SASH

This lovely design of groups of patterns embodies the Japanese sense of harmony. (See photo page 141.)

OUTLINE: diamonds, flames and flames with stripes

STITCH LENGTH: covering 4 threads

STEPS: up or down 2 threads

COLORS: 4. See color page 67. If you prefer a patchwork effect, use 4 colors of different combinations in each of the 5 patterns.

A. Start at the right edge of the canvas.

B. Make the outline of a diamond (arrow):
    Asc. and desc. 6 single sts. *each side*.

NOTE: Complete the outline of each pattern, working from the right to left across the canvas. They are separated by a single vertical stripe.

C. Flames with stripe: Flames—asc. and desc. 6 single sts.
    Stripes pierce the top and bottom points of the flame.

D. Diamonds: Asc. and desc. 4 dbl. sts. *each side*.

E. Reverse C.

F. Flames: Asc. and desc. 5 dbl. sts.

G. Repeat C.

H. Repeat from B across the canvas. Carry on.

# 40 ✍

# ADAPTED FROM ITALIAN
# SEVENTEENTH-CENTURY CEILING

This beautiful design is most challenging to execute, with a great variety of stitch combinations.

OUTLINE: large (circle-like) hexagons and small (rectangular) hexagons

STITCH LENGTH: covering 2 and 4 threads*

STEPS: up or down 0 and 2 threads

COLORS: 3. 4 grad. of 1st color; 3 grad. of 2nd color; 2 grad. of 3rd color. See color page 75.

* The top left of the photograph illustrates the use of stitch length (covering 2 and 4) in the outline and the design of the fill.

A. Start in the center of the canvas. This is the center stitch of the horizontal line in the large hexagon.

B. Make the outline of a large hexagon (arrow):
1. Horizontal line: 17 sts. These stitches alternate 1 long (covering 4) with 2 short (covering 2), one on top of the other.
2. Diagonals: 4 dbl. sts.
3. Verticals: 4 groups of 3 sts.
   Alternate stitch placement in each repeat (the shorts are over the longs).

C. Outline the small hexagons—(covering 2, steps–0)
   Horizontal line—19 sts.

D. Complete the outlines and fill in all remaining areas as shown.

NOTE: In the horizontal lines of the large hexagon, do not stitch short stitches one on top of the other; rather work short stitches clear across the canvas and then back again, to achieve the placement.

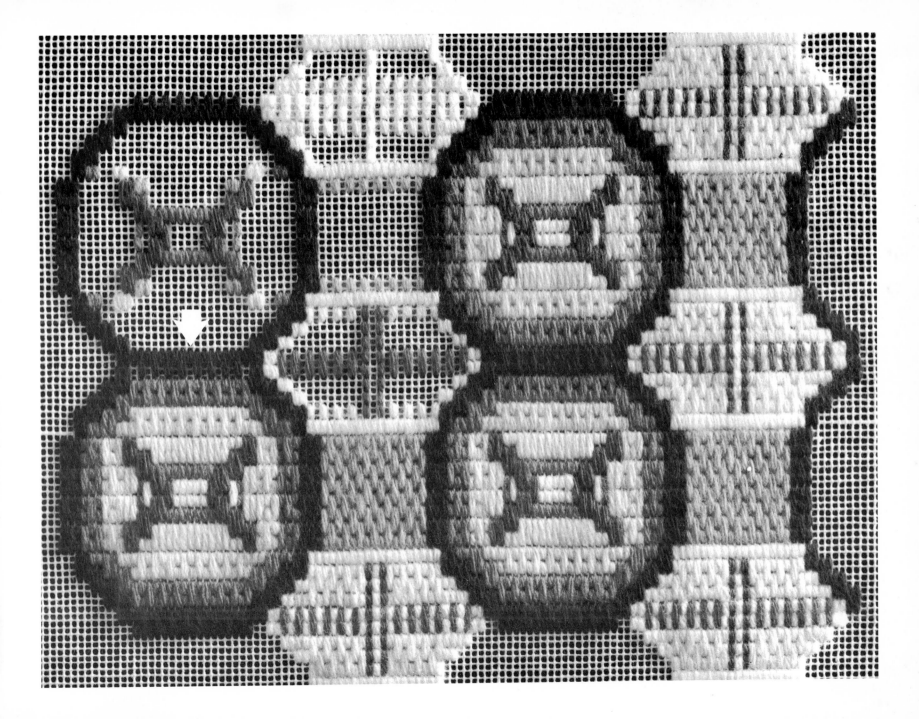

# 41 ✒

## ADAPTED FROM GERMAN
## FIFTEENTH-CENTURY LACE

This delicious design comes from the Collection Brockhaus, Germany.

OUTLINE: large dark diamonds

STITCH LENGTH: outline—covering 4 threads
interior design—covering 2, 3 and 4 threads

STEPS: outline—up or down 2 threads
interior design—up or down 1 and 2 threads

COLORS: 4. See color page 70.

A. Start from the center of the canvas, count up 20 holes.
B. Make the outline of a diamond (arrow):
Asc. and desc. 12 dbl. sts. *each side.*
C. When the canvas is covered with diamond outlines, make an inner row within the diamonds.
D. Make the interior design.

NOTE: The small diamonds at the vertical points of the large diamonds (illustrated in the upper middle of the photograph) are different from the small diamonds at the horizontal points of the large diamond (illustrated on the left side of the photograph).

# 42 ✒

# INSPIRED BY PERUVIAN (CENTRAL COAST) INCA PERIOD TAPESTRY

The tapestry with interlocking snakes, which inspired this smart design, is to be found in the Robert Woods Bliss Collection (National Gallery of Art, Washington, D.C.) and it dates between 1450–1535 A.D.

OUTLINE: flame

STITCH LENGTH: covering 4 threads

STEPS: up or down 2 threads

COLORS: 5 or more. You can do this in a great variety of colors. If you use graded colors be sure they are not too close in tone or you will lose the design. See color page 71.

SPECIAL PROJECTS: vest (men or women)

A. Start in the center of the canvas, with the high point of the flame.

B. Make the outline of a flame (arrow). Insert 1st stitch then:
   1. Desc. lt. 5 sts.
   2. Desc. rt. 2 sts.
   3. Desc. lt. 4 sts.
   4. Desc. rt. 2 sts.
   5. Desc. lt. 5 sts. (low point)
   Repeat 1–5 substituting asc. for desc.

C. Repeat B across the canvas and above and below. Carry on and complete as shown.

# 43 ✍

## ADAPTED FROM AMERICAN EIGHTEENTH-TO EARLY-NINETEENTH-CENTURY JACQUARD WEAVE FABRIC

This classic design is from a coverlet in the Collection of The Colonial Coverlet Guild of America.

OUTLINE: diamonds and 3-peak motif
STITCH LENGTH: covering 4 threads, except in the small motif—covering 2* and 4 threads
STEPS: up or down 2 threads
COLORS: 5. 3 grad. each of 2 colors; 2 grad. of 3rd color; 2 single colors (each for the centers of the diamonds and small motifs). See color page 66.

A. Start from the center of the canvas, count up 12 holes.
B. Make the outline of a diamond (arrow):
　　Asc. and desc. 8 dbl. sts. *each side*.
C. Outline the 3-peak motif—make them at the horizontal points of the diamonds.
D. Complete as shown.

NOTE: You have automatically outlined the row of small motifs by repeating the row of diamonds and 3-peak motifs.

* The left side of the photograph shows the location of all stitches covering 2 threads.

# 44 ✍

## INSPIRED BY CHINESE EIGHTEENTH-CENTURY MANDARIN COSTUME

The costume on which I found this marvelous design is presently in the Collection of the Telfair Academy, Savannah, Georgia.

OUTLINE: 3-arch motif (full arch plus its side arches)

STITCH LENGTH: outline—covering 6 threads (except as described below in NOTE)

fill—covering 2, 4 and 6 threads*

STEPS: up or down 2 threads

COLORS: 6. 3 grad. of 1st color; 2 grad. each of next 4 colors; single grade of 6th color. See color page 76.

* The left side of the photograph shows the location of all stitches covering 2 and 4 threads.

A. Start in the center of the canvas. This is the center stitch at the top of the full arch.

B. Make the outline of a full arch (arrow).

C. Make the outline of a side arch on either side of the full arch.

NOTE: The top of the 1st dark stitch group (covering 4), of the side arch, is in the same horiz. line as that of the adjoining stitch group of the full arch.

D. Work in a mirror image—the 3-arch motif (C, B, C) across the canvas.

NOTE: A stitch covering 2 separates C and D.

E. Fill as shown.

# 45 🖋

# INSPIRED BY FRENCH
# EIGHTEENTH-CENTURY PALACE FLOORS

The magnificent parquet floors of Versailles and the Hôtel de Soubise, Paris, inspired this design.

Turn the book around so that the stitches in the photograph are vertical.

OUTLINE: diamonds

STITCH LENGTH: covering 4 threads

STEPS: up or down 2 threads

COLORS: flame—6. 2 grad. each of 5 colors; single grade of 6th color
      intersecting lines—6. 3 grad. of 1st color; 2 grad. each of the next
           3 colors; single grade of 5th and 6th colors, for
           the background. See color page 72.

A. Start from the center of the canvas, count to the right 19 holes.

B. Make the outline of a diamond (arrow):
      Asc. and desc. 20 sts. *each side.*

C. Cover the canvas with diamond outlines.

D. Then fill with the flame motifs and the intersecting lines.

CHECK PHOTOGRAPH: The colors of the flame motifs alternate horizontally
      as do the intersecting line motifs.

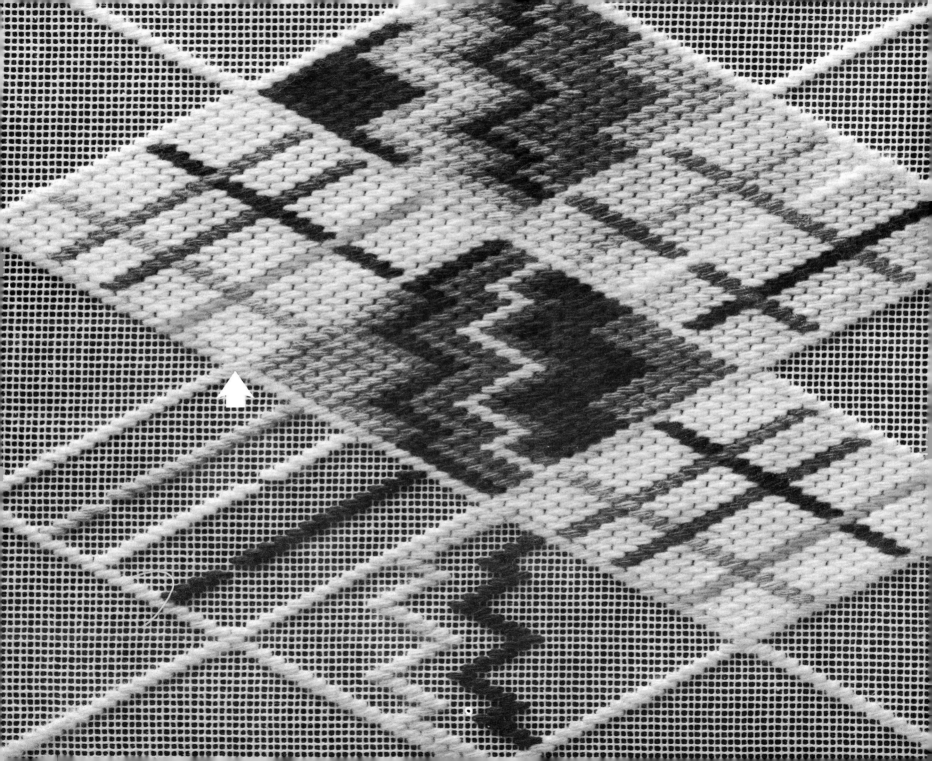

# 46 ✍

## INSPIRED BY JAPANESE (OKINAWA)
## EIGHTEENTH-CENTURY TEXTILE

This design was inspired by Japanese landscape and is very beautiful. (See photo page 141.)

OUTLINE: foreground and background mountains
STITCH LENGTH: outlines—covering 4 threads
                fill     —covering 2* and 4 threads
STEPS: up or down 2 threads
COLORS: 7 or more. In my selection of colors I used my colors freely. One could use one's leftover wools, repeating or not as one pleases and create a rich and colorful patchwork effect. See color page 80.

A. Start from the center of the canvas, count to the left 4 holes.
B. Make the outline of a foreground mountain (arrow).
C. Make the outline of a background mountain on either side of the foreground mountain.
D. Make B and C across the canvas, then above and below.
E. Carry on and complete as shown.

* All stitches covering 2 threads are located in the row directly below the outline of B and C. See the upper left of the photograph.

# 47 ✍

# INSPIRED BY CENTRAL AFRICAN PAINTING IN INTAGLIO ON A WOODEN UTENSIL

This design, from the Louvre Museum, Paris, invokes the thoughts of a mysterious jungle.

OUTLINE: large (dark) and small (light) diamonds
STITCH LENGTH: covering 4 threads
STEPS: up or down 2 threads
COLORS: 4. 4 grad. of 1st color; 3 grad. of 2nd color; 2 grad. of 3rd color; single grade of 4th color.

NOTE: The gradations of light colors should alternate horizontally with the gradations of dark colors. See color page 74.

A. Start from the center of the canvas, count to the right 28 holes.
B. Make the outline of a large diamond (arrow):
    Asc. and desc. 29 sts. *each side.*
C. Cover the canvas with large diamond outlines.
D. Make an inner row within each large diamond outline.
E. Between the horiz. pts. of the large diamond, make 7 small diamonds:
    Asc. and desc. 4 sts. *each side.*
F. Repeat the rows above and below the small diamonds until the canvas is filled.

# 48 ✍

# INSPIRED BY SIBERIAN
# NINETEENTH-CENTURY
# BRIDAL COAT EMBROIDERY

The coat inspiring this sophisticated design is to be found in the American Museum of Natural History, New York. (See photo page 143.)

Turn the book around so that all the stitches in the photograph are vertical.

OUTLINE: onion motif
STITCH LENGTH: outline—covering 4 threads
          fill     —covering 2* and 4 threads
STEPS: up or down 1 thread
COLORS: 7. See color page 75.
SPECIAL PROJECTS: ladies bolero or vest, upholstery

* The upper right of the photograph shows the location of all stitches, covering 2 threads.

A. Start in the center of the canvas. This is the high point of the onion motif.
B. Make the outline of an onion motif (arrow). Insert 1st stitch, then:

| Desc. lt. | 1. 3 singles | 6. 1 quadruple |
|---|---|---|
| | 2. 2 doubles | 7. 2 triples |
| | 3. 2 triples | 8. 2 doubles |
| | 4. 1 quadruple | 9. 4 singles |
| | 5. 1 quintuple | |

Desc. lt. 1–9
Asc. rt. then lt. repeating 1–9.

C. Cover the canvas with onion motif outlines.
D. When filling note the first 4 colors are each composed of 2 rows; the 5th, 6th and 7th colors are each composed of 3 rows.

# 49 ✍

# INSPIRED BY FRANK STELLA
# PAINTING "TUXEDO PARK"

This design is so contemporary. The squares that automatically appear give it an op-art effect.

Turn the book around so that the stitches in the photograph are vertical.

OUTLINE: dark diamonds

STITCH LENGTH: dark diamonds—covering 2 threads

               light diamonds—covering 4 threads, except the horizontal point covers 2, and the 3rd stitch from the horizontal point covers 6.*

STEPS: dark diamonds—up or down 1 thread

     light diamonds—up or down 3 threads

COLORS: 2. See color page 69.

SPECIAL PROJECTS: all types of upholstery, handbag

A. Start from the center of the canvas, count to the left 45 holes.
B. Make the outline of a dark diamond (arrow):
    Asc. and desc. 46 sts. *each side.*
C. Cover the canvas with outlines of dark diamonds.
D. Fill with alternate light and dark diamonds.

* The top of the right side of the photograph shows the location of all stitches, covering 6 threads.

# 50 ✑

## ADAPTED FROM NIGERIA (YORUBA)
## BRASS KNIFE BLADE

This striking design is etched on the blade of a saber in the American Museum of Natural History, New York. (See photo page 140.)

OUTLINE: diagonals from the center and diamonds

STITCH LENGTH: covering 3 threads

except 1) diamond—horizontal point covers 2* and the stitch before the horizontal point covers 4.*

2) diagonals from the diamond edge to the canvas edge (see the bottom of the photograph) covers 2,* 3 and 4.*

STEPS: up or down 2 threads

COLORS: 3. 2 single colors; 3 grad. of 3rd color. I have used 1 strand from each of these 3 grades and put them together to create a beautiful multishaded color in the 5th, 6th, and 7th rows inside the diamond. See color page 66.

NOTE: This design is made in a mitre form. Start in the center and turn the canvas each time you work in the direction of another edge.

A. Start in the center of the canvas with a single stitch (covering 4). Shown in a light color for easy identification (arrow).

B. Make 4 diagonal lines—extending from the center stitch to the 4 corners.

C. Repeat the diagonals for 2 more rows.

D. Make the outline of the diamonds: Asc. and desc. 29 sts. *each side*.

E. Fill diamonds.

F. Make the diagonals from the diamond edge to the canvas edge.

NOTE: In even rows, the 1st stitch next to the diamond covers 2, the 2nd stitch covers 4. The rest cover 3.
In odd rows all stitches cover 3.

* The left side of the photograph shows the location of all stitches covering 2 and 4 threads.

# 51 ✍

## ADAPTED FROM CHINESE
## SECOND- TO THIRD-CENTURY SILK
## (FOUND IN A PALMYRA TOMB)

Aesthetically I prefer this elegant design, once completed, with stitches placed horizontally.

OUTLINE: motifs

STITCH LENGTH: covers 4 threads

STEPS: up or down 2 threads

COLORS: 4. The outline made in a darker grade of the background color. Motifs of the same color are created in diagonal rows descending from left to right. See color page 78.

SPECIAL PROJECTS: upholstery for dining chairs

A. Start from the center of the canvas, count down 38 holes.

B. Make a motif (arrow). Insert 1st stitch, then:

| | | | |
|---|---|---|---|
| 1. Desc. lt. 17 sts. | | 4. Desc. rt. 8 sts. |
| 2. Asc. lt. 5 sts. | | 5. Asc. rt. 5 sts. |
| 3. Desc. lt. 8 sts. | | 6. Desc. rt. 17 sts. |

Turn the canvas upside down, repeat 1–6.

C. To mark the distance between motifs:

Vertically—insert 7 sts. (temporary).

Horizontally—insert 11 sts. (temporary).

D. Make a new motif. Follow B.

E. Cover the canvas with outline motifs, carry on.

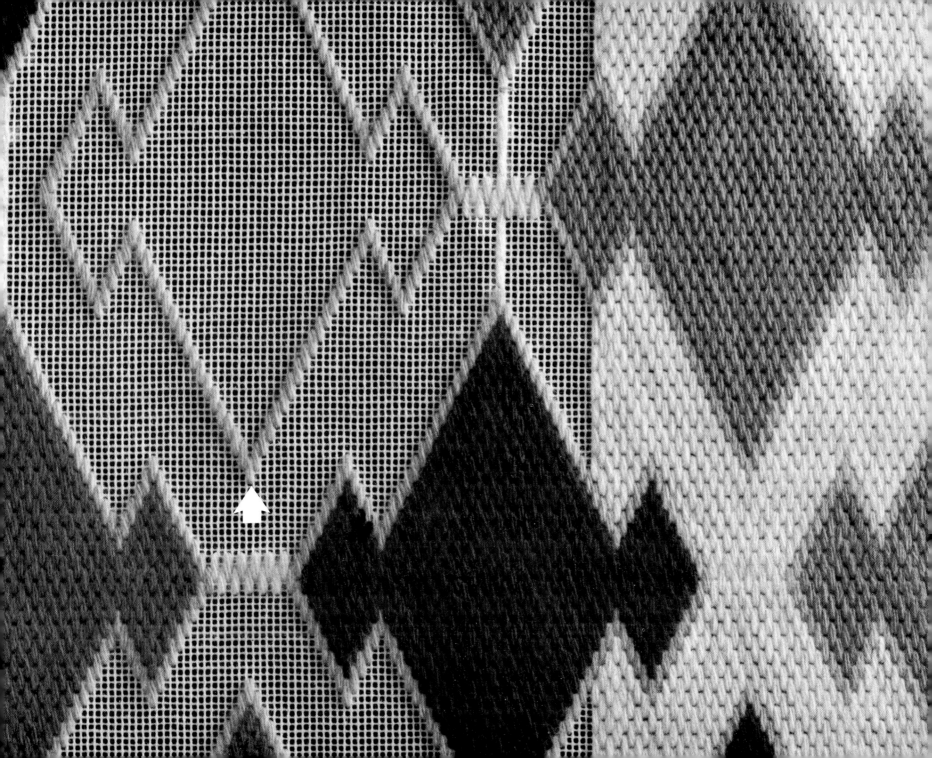

## 52 ⚞

## ADAPTED FROM GERMAN
## SAMPLER, CIRCA 1688

The sampler from which this bold design comes is in the Victoria and Albert Museum, London.

Turn the book around so that the stitches in the photograph are vertical.

OUTLINE: diamonds
STITCH LENGTH:covering 4 threads
STEPS: up or down 2 threads
COLORS: 6. See color page 65.

A. Start from the center of the canvas count up 36 holes.
B. Make the outline of a diamond (arrow):
    Asc. and desc. 20 dbl. sts. *each side*.
C. Cover the canvas with diamond outlines.
D. Cover the canvas with an inner row in the same color.
E. Fill in the rest of the diamonds as shown.

## 53 ✍

# ADAPTED FROM LOWER CONGO
# WOVEN BASKET

This stunning design was originally used on an ornamental basket which now belongs to the Musée Royal de l'Afrique Centrale, Tervuren, Belgium.

Turn the book around so that the stitches in the photographs are vertical.

OUTLINE: largest dark outline of the motif shown
STITCH LENGTH: covering 4 threads
STEPS: up or down 2 threads
COLORS: 4. See color page 71.

A. Start in the center of the canvas.

B. Make the outline of a motif (arrow):
Long sides: Asc. and desc. 24 sts. *each side.*
Medium sides: Asc. and desc. 15 sts. *each side.*
Short sides: Asc. and desc. 10 sts. *each side.*

NOTE: The medium sides of the motif are also the medium sides of the adjoining motifs (below to the right and left).
The short sides of the motif are also the last 10 stitches of the long sides of the motifs above or below.

C. Cover the canvas with motif outlines, and carry on.

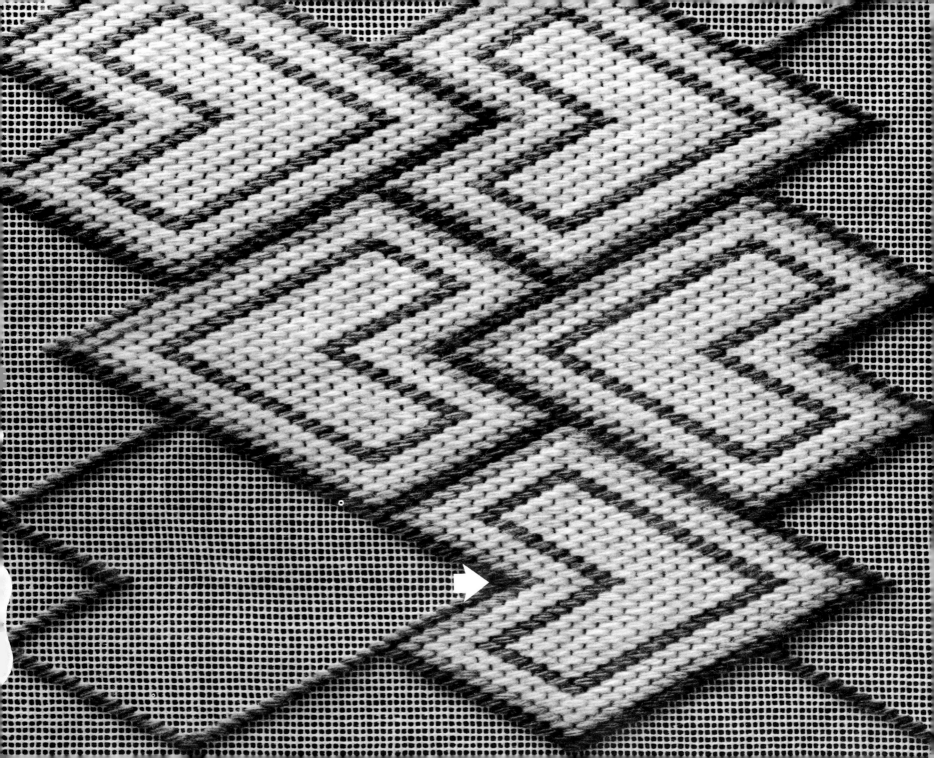

# 54 🖉

## INSPIRED BY NEW ENGLAND EIGHTEENTH-CENTURY HAND-WOVEN COVERLET

The coverlet containing this interesting design is presently in the Newark Museum, Newark, New Jersey.

Turn the book around so that the stitches in the photograph are vertical.

OUTLINE: large diamonds with 2 inverted corners
STITCH LENGTH: covering 4 threads
STEPS: up or down 2 threads
COLORS: 3. 2 grad. each of 2 colors; single grade of 3rd color. See color page 65.

A. Start from the center of the canvas, count to the right 1 hole.
B. Make the outline of a large diamond (arrow):
    Long sides: Asc. and desc. 14 dbl. sts. *each side*.
    Inverted corners: Asc. and desc. 3 dbl. sts. *each side*.

NOTE: The location of the inverted corners, outlining the small light diamonds, occur at the vertical points of one large diamond and at the horizontal points of the adjoining large diamond.

C. Cover the canvas with large diamond outlines.
D. Fill in the large and small diamonds as shown.

## 55 ✍

# INSPIRED BY TURKISH (KONYA)
# THIRTEENTH-CENTURY SELJUK TILE PANEL

This beautiful and complex design dates from 1251–52 and by order of the Emir Celaduddin Karatay, a vizer of Key Karus II, decorated a religious school. (See photo page 143.)

In order to create this design in Bargello, I had to return to basic geometric shapes, which the Seljuks were masters at hiding in complicated patterns.

STITCH LENGTH: covering 2 and 4 threads
STEPS: up or down 2 threads
COLORS: 3. 2 grad. each of 2 colors, single grade 1 color—border and horizontal stripes. See color page 65.
SPECIAL PROJECTS: this would make a sensational cornice.

I feel this is the most complex design in this book. The photograph is really clearer than any written instructions. It is left unexplained leaving the challenge and fun to you.

One can make this design as long as one desires. I like a wide border surrounding it. I also think the scale of this design is more effective when worked on a no. 12 canvas.

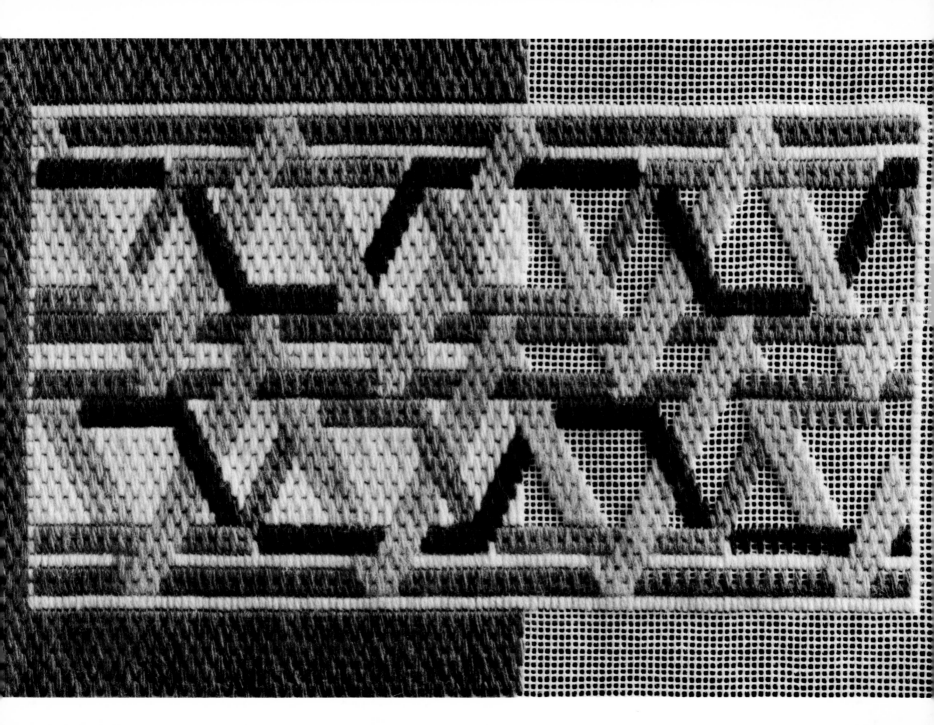

# 56 ✍

## ADAPTED FROM WEST AFRICAN
## (BUSHONGA TRIBE)
## EIGHTEENTH-CENTURY WOVEN RAFFIA

This marvelous design dates back to the eighteenth century or earlier and the raffia is very finely woven. It is presently in the British Museum, London.

Turn the book around so that the stitches in the photograph are vertical.

OUTLINE: impossible to isolate (see arrow)

STITCH LENGTH: covering 4 threads, except at the top and bottom edge of the background—short (cover 2) alternate with long (cover 4)

STEPS: up or down 2 threads

COLORS: 4. 4 grad. each of 1st and 2nd color; single grades for the background and border. See color page 74.

SPECIAL PROJECTS: wall hanging, tennis racket cover, photo album cover

A. Start from the center of the canvas, count up 32 holes.

B. Make the outline of the motif (arrow):

|  |  |  |  |  |  |  |  |  |
|---|---|---|---|---|---|---|---|---|
|  | 1. Asc. | rt. | 12 dbl. sts. |  | 13. Desc. lt. | 4 dbl. sts. |
|  | 2. Desc. | rt. | 10 dbl. sts. |  | 14. Desc. rt. | 8 dbl. sts. |
|  | 3. Desc. | lt. | 18 dbl. sts. |  | 15. Skip 4* |  |
|  | 4. Skip 4* |  |  |  | CHANGE COLOR |  |
| Cont. | 5. Desc. lt. | | 16 dbl. sts. | Cont. | 16. Desc. rt. | 10 dbl. sts. |
|  | 6. Desc. rt. | | 4 dbl. sts. |  | 17. Skip 4* |  |
|  | 7. Asc. rt. | | 8 dbl. sts. | Cont. | 18. Desc. rt. | 12 dbl. sts. |
|  | 8. Skip 4* |  |  |  | 19. Desc. lt. | 10 dbl. sts. |
| Cont. | 9. Asc. rt. | | 11 dbl. sts. |  | 20. Asc. lt. | 18 dbl. sts. |
|  | 10. Asc. lt. | | 3 dbl. sts. |  | 21. Skip 4* |  |
|  | 11. Skip 4* |  |  | Cont. | 22. Asc. lt. | 7 dbl. sts. |
| Cont. | 12. Asc. lt. | | 16 dbl. sts. |  | 23. Asc. rt. | 13 dbl. sts. |

C. Add 3 rows. Begin these rows just under the stitch indicated by the arrow.

Repeat B 1–23.

D. Make the background within and without the motif, then the border.

* To avoid a miscount, insert (temporarily) 4 dbls. in another color.

# 57 ✍

## ADAPTED FROM FRENCH
## ENAMEL CIGARETTE CASE, CIRCA 1930

This sophisticated design is absolutely a summary of the Art Deco style.

OUTLINE: total linear part of the design

STITCH LENGTH: triangles—covering 4 threads, except stitches just above base, and base–1 long (cover 4) alternating with 2 short (cover 2) stitches, one on top of the other.

STEPS: up or down 2 threads

COLORS: 5. Single grades each of 4 colors; 2 grades of 5th color. See color page 80.

SPECIAL PROJECTS: this would be most effective as a panel on an attaché case or an evening bag.

A. Start at the bottom near the right edge of the canvas.

B. Make the outer triangle (arrow):
   Asc. lt. 47 sts.
   Desc. lt. 46 sts.      Make the base.

C. Make the inner triangle–from the arrow, count to the left 18 stitches. Start in the hole above. 1st stitch short then:
   Asc. lt. 29 sts.
   Desc. lt. 29 sts. (last stitch short)

D. Complete the linear pattern as shown, and carry on.

129

## 58 ✍

# ADAPTED FROM PENNSYLVANIAN EIGHTEENTH-CENTURY NEEDLEPOINT MEDALLION

This striking design is from the 1723 Morris family Bible which still belongs to the family.

A. Start from the center of the canvas, count up 40 holes.

B. Make the outline of the medallion (arrow). Insert 1st stitch, then:

| | | | |
|---|---|---|---|
| 1. Desc. lt. 4 dbl. sts. | | 9. Desc. lt. 4 dbl. sts. | |
| 2. Asc. lt. 4 dbl. sts. | | 10. Desc. rt. 6 dbl. sts. | |
| 3. Desc. lt. 6 dbl. sts. | | 11. Asc. rt. 3 dbl. sts. | |
| 4. Desc. rt. 3 dbl. sts. | | 12. Desc. rt. 5 dbl. sts. | |
| 5. Desc. lt. 5 dbl. sts. | | 13. Desc. lt. 3 dbl. sts. | |
| 6. Asc. lt. 3 dbl. sts. | | 14. Desc. rt. 6 dbl. sts. | |
| 7. Desc. lt. 6 dbl. sts. | | 15. Asc. rt. 4 dbl. sts. | |
| 8. Desc. rt. 4 dbl. sts. | | 16. Desc. rt. 4 dbl. sts. | |

Turn the canvas upside down and repeat 1–16.

C. Fill the medallion and make the background as shown.

OUTLINE: outermost row of the design

STITCH LENGTH: up or down 2 threads

COLORS: 5. 3 grad. each of 1st, 2nd and 3rd colors; single grades of 4th and 5th colors. See color page 80.

NOTE: You can use this as a solitary medallion or leave a space of 4 inches between each medallion horizontally and vertically.

## 59 ✍

# ADAPTED FROM NORTHWEST MEXICAN TRADITIONAL WOVEN SERAPE

This stunning design is so vibrant.

Turn the book around so that the stitches in the photograph are vertical.

OUTLINE: outermost row of design

STITCH LENGTH: covering 4 threads

STEPS: up or down 2 threads

COLORS: 5. 2 grad. each of 1st and 2nd colors; single grades of 3rd, 4th and 5th colors. Use 2 bright colors, surrounded each time by a very dark color or black. This creates a dynamic effect as shown on color page 78.

SPECIAL PROJECTS: upholstery, ottoman or footstool

A. Start from the center of the canvas, count up 64 holes.

B. Make the outline of the medallion (arrow). Insert 1st stitch, then:

| | | |
|---|---|---|
| 1. Desc. lt. 6 sts. | 8. Desc. rt. 20 sts. | |
| 2. Asc. lt. 4 sts. | 9. Asc. rt. 3 sts. | |
| 3. Desc. lt. 9 sts. | 10. Desc. rt. 9 sts. | |
| 4. Asc. lt. 4 sts. | 11. Asc. rt. 4 sts. | |
| 5. Desc. lt. 9 sts. | 12. Desc. rt. 9 sts. | |
| 6. Asc. lt. 3 sts. | 13. Asc. rt. 4 sts. | |
| 7. Desc. lt. 20 sts. | 14. Desc. rt. 6 sts. | |

Turn the canvas upside down and repeat 1–14.

C. Fill as shown.

NOTE: You can keep enlarging this design to desired size by adding as many rows as you need, or you can treat it as a medallion and make a solid background around it.

# 60 ✒

# ADAPTED FROM AMERICAN
# TRADITIONAL QUILT

This handsome design is a standout anywhere.

OUTLINE: four dark diagonals from the center

STITCH LENGTH: covering 4 threads

STEPS: up or down 2 threads

COLORS: 7. It is most striking to make the outline row dark, the 4th row from the outline dark, and the last 2 rows light. See color page 67.

SPECIAL PROJECTS: makes excellent squares for a rug (reverse colors in alternate squares)

A. Start in the center of the canvas.

B. Make the 4 dark center diagonals (arrow):
   1. 1st diagonal—Asc. rt. to edge.
   2. 2nd diagonal—Asc. lt. to edge.
   3. 3rd diagonal—Desc. rt. to edge.
   4. 4th diagonal—Desc. lt. to edge.

NOTE: When starting the 3rd and 4th diagonal, check the photograph carefully, as they start to the left of the center (1st) stitch.

C. To the right (clockwise) of each dark center diagonal make 6 rows of different colors extending to the edge of the canvas.

D. To the left (counterclockwise) of the dark center diagonals make 6 more rows.

NOTE: Always keep the colors in the same order.

E. Make the background.

# 61 ✍

## ADAPTED FROM JAVANESE NINETEENTH-CENTURY BATIK

This design has great strength.

OUTLINE: largest diamond and rows
STITCH LENGTH: covering 2* and 4 threads
STEPS: up or down 2 threads
COLORS: 2. See color page 79.
SPECIAL PROJECTS: Makes excellent squares for a rug.

* The stitches covering 2 threads are all located just outside the diamond outline. See the lower part of the photograph.

A. Start from the center of the canvas, count up 24 holes.
B. Make the outline of the diamond (arrow):
   Asc. and desc. 14 dbl. sts. *each side*.
C. Make rows starting from the vert. pts. of the diamond and work to the edge until the canvas is covered.
D. Fill the diamond.

VARIATION: Repeat the diamond again:
   Horizontally: After 20 rows.
   Vertically: After 10 rows.

## 62 ✁
## ADAPTED FROM NAVAHO
## TRADITIONAL RUG

The stitch technique of this beautiful design gives the effect of corduroy.

OUTLINE: groups of vertical stitches
STITCH LENGTH: covering 6 threads
STEPS: up or down 6 threads
COLORS: 9 or more. See color page 84.
SPECIAL PROJECTS: covers for telephone book, photo album, etc.

A. Make a triple (3 stitches) in the center of the canvas (arrow).
B. To the right and left of the center triple—make (group of) 6 sts.
C. Immediately above and below the center triple—make (group of) 9 sts.
D. Immediately above and below C—make (group of) 3 sts.
   Build out as shown.

NOTE: At the vertical points, 3 stitches alternate with 9.

VARIATION: See p. 6.

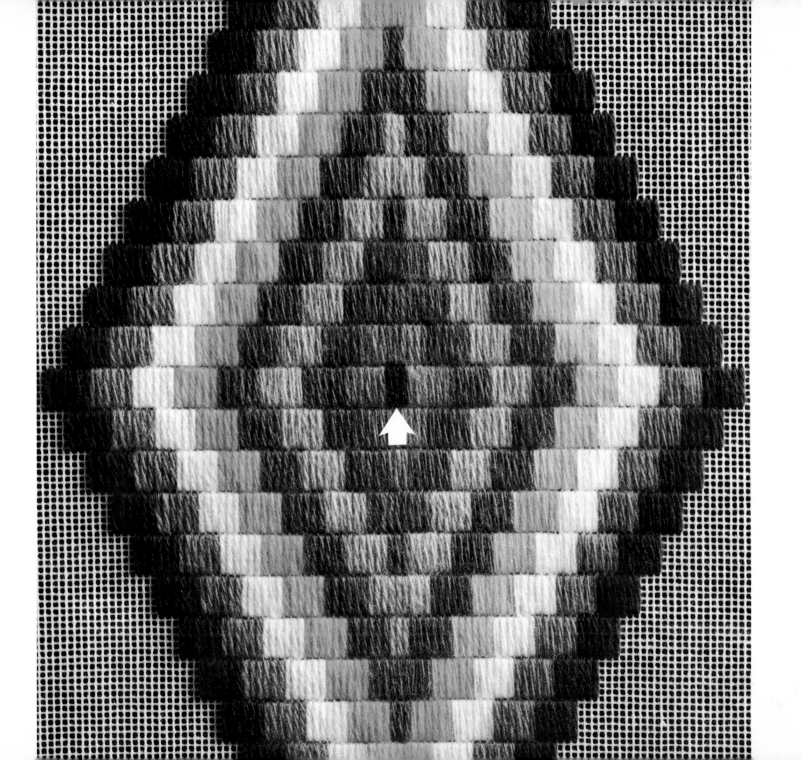

# SOME SOURCES AND
# THE DESIGNS ADAPTED FROM THEM

*Nigeria Knife Blade Ornament*

*Design 50*

*Turkish Brickwork Thirteenth Century*

*Design 11*

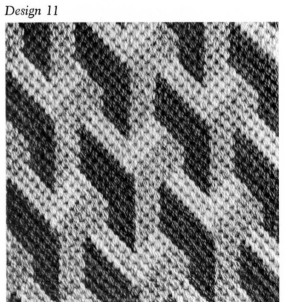

*Japanese Traditional Sash*

Design 39

*Japanese Textile Eighteenth Century*
Design 46

*Italian Lace Nineteenth Century*
*Design 15*

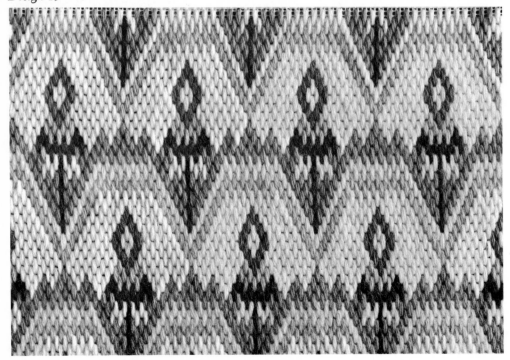

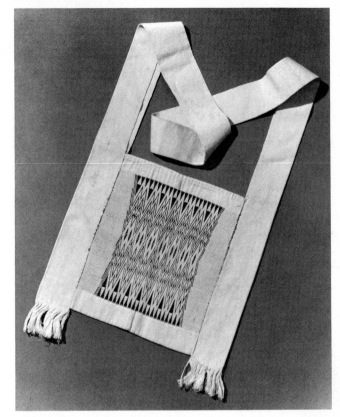

*Indian Shambag Twentieth Century*
*Design 2*

Turkish Tile Thirteenth Century
Design 55

Siberian
Embroidery
Nineteenth
Century

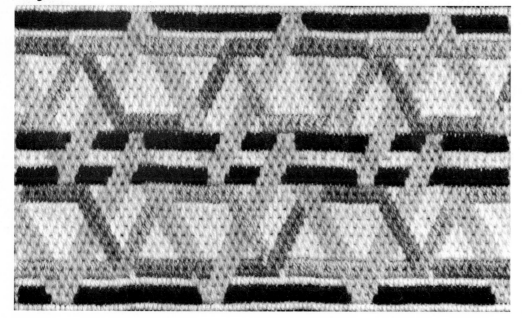

Design 48

143

If you do not know the location of the closest supplier of fine needle-work canvas and yarn, write either of the following firms and they will send you this information.

Wholesale Supplier of Paterna-Persian yarn and canvas:

Paternayan Bros.
312 East 95th Street
New York, New York 10028

Wholesale Supplier of tapestry, crewel yarn and canvas:

Joan Toggitt
1170 Broadway (Room 406)
New York, New York 10001

In New York there are many fine art needleworks shops; one of them is:

Selma's Art Needlework
1645 Second Avenue (between 85th and 86th streets)
New York, New York 10028

They carry Paterna-Persian, as well as other tapestry yarns, and very good canvas.

I have my pillows made by:

Alexander and Fischer
1483 Second Avenue
New York, New York 10021

For fine needlework mounting, I suggest:

Martha Klein Handbags Ltd.
3785 Broadway
New York, New York 10032